Coffee Table Coloring Book

*...featuring the resiliency
and beauty of the people of Nepal...*

by Kenny Reese Allen

First, I exhibit in black and white, 26 of my favorite personal photos of our eight trips into Nepal and then offer you texturized images in the second half of the book for adding color as you wish. I believe this will be both informative and therapeutic, across all age groups as you identify with the poor of Nepal and sense their incredible resiliency.

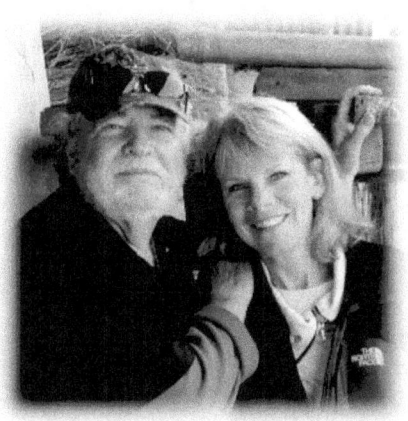

Kenny and Vicky Allen

"You do well if you really fulfill the royal law according to the Scripture, 'You shall love your neighbor as yourself.' But if you show partiality, you commit sin" (James 2:8–9).

The sin is that when we favor the rich and powerful, we are serving ourselves rather than others. This is because the rich and powerful have the potential to bestow a bit of their riches and power on us. The poor can do nothing for us. But they are the people in need.

———————————————

"One who is gracious to a poor man lends to the LORD,

And He will repay him for his good deed." Proverbs 19:17

My awakening to art...

In college, way back, I chose two electives in my last semester and those were photography and ad layout and design, but never intended it would be vocational, and so far has not been. I thoroughly enjoyed these classes and have had the opportunity to apply the knowledge gained in many ways. I was fascinated as to how visual images impacted lives especially after reading a text book on subliminal advertising.

Fast forward to 2011 when I began to work with visually reformatting some of my travel photos, my favorites being those of developing countries like, Nepal and Sumatra. That was when I began connecting more fully with the detailed setting of each photo by applying my own color and texture and sketching. In fact, I began an art page on my website and my friends began to take notice. I named my proprietary technique "photo/sketch/art." Through this I immersed in detail that I had never seen before and much more appreciated the minutia like; tattered clothing, unmatched shoes, scarce nutrition, hard labor, family unity and much more. It was an emotive and spiritual experience especially when I looked more closely at the plight of the profoundly poor.

As a Christian, my hope for this publication is multifaceted; 1) that there will be a stirring of hearts toward the poor 2) that art would be embraced as a way of re-coloring the fabric of God's wonderful creation 3) that many would recognize and be bold enough to display their talent for art and offer their work for others to enjoy 4) and that, young people in particular, would rise above a western mentality where they can *easily become ungrateful for all that they have if they remain isolated from the poor and as to how they might help them.*

An excerpt from the book, "Every Good Endeavor" by Timothy Keller helped me see art as a calling that can be known as a work prepared in advance, by God, for so many who may have ignored its powerful impact on changing our culture for the good, His good. The crux of the writing went something like this: To anyone who is a visual artist, does Christian teaching about the nature of reality bear on what they depict and how they display that through their art? Will their art be influenced by their beliefs about sin and redemption and hope for the future? It seems that it must. Finally, is their art a way of letting others know of their Christian faith and help them understand that their work is an act of service to God and neighbors rather than a way to get self-esteem and status? Does the same apply to writing and publishing and music and dance and painting and photography and ultimately in all the arts? I believe so.

Anyway, I am all in and hope to continue to refine all of my work in my life into a tapestry which, although I may never fully see, or understand in the present, will bring glory to God. KRA

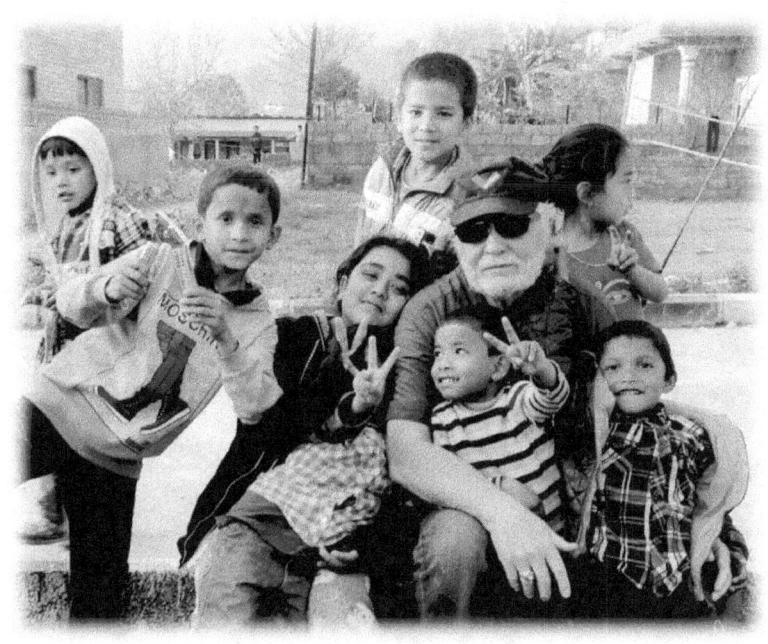

This is my favorite photo of the neighborhood kids near our seasonal apartment in Pokhara, Nepal. Shortly hereafter I began to form a club we named Team Orange because of the color of the rubber gloves we gave each member to use when picking up trash and, as a reward, giving fresh oranges to each team member after the work was complete. Then, we cooked open-air style serving hot vegetable soup to the team and others. Afterward, they all played volleyball with donated equipment as an adult volunteer supervised. The plan is, upon returning, to expand the clubs into other neighborhoods and initiate tutoring in English and math and disciplines toward character development.

Why the book?

Many are saying that coloring is therapeutic and I believe that. This coffee-table book offers a creative way to impart to hearts and minds "hands on" details of many in Nepal who, for one reason or another, often by no fault of their own, are profoundly poor but have remained resilient in their efforts to overcome arduous situations. By literally adding your color to these textured prints in the back, you will be able to touch the details and minutia of their settings, more so than if you just quickly glanced at a photo. You will be considering the poor, and God says we are to do that. Perhaps for you, this is about your children who need to be made more aware of the poor. Also, by visibly placing this on your coffee table, you may inspire those who visit your home, or office.

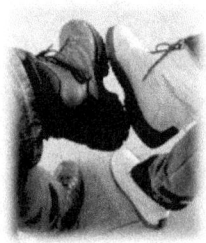 *Personally speaking, after visiting several developing countries over the past few years, Vicky and I believe that the best way to help the poor is to be there yourself, if possible, or support those in the regions who are trustworthy "boots on the ground" people.*

This publication helps Vicky and I and those in Nepal because, although there are only small royalties in self publishing, each purchase of this book sends dollars into a special account in the USA that helps us return to Nepal to continue serving where we have credible, trustworthy relationships. My next coloring book may highlight the indigenous people of Ecuador.

Sincerely,

Kenny Reese Allen

WEBSITE - www.kennyreeseallen.com

EMAIL – coffeetablecoloringbook@gmail.com

About our work in Nepal...

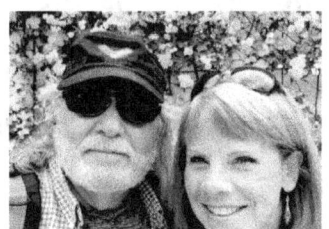

We first visited Nepal in the summer of 2011 as raw tourists who had learned from our teaching colleagues in the UAE that flights were cheap and the town of Pokhara was the place to slow down and experience a picturesque region they call "The Rooftop of the World." Since 2011, Vicky and I have returned seven times to Pokhara and with each departure, we have increased longings to return as soon as able.

It took us very little time to discover kind and caring people everywhere we went, in the tourist shops, in the restaurants, in the

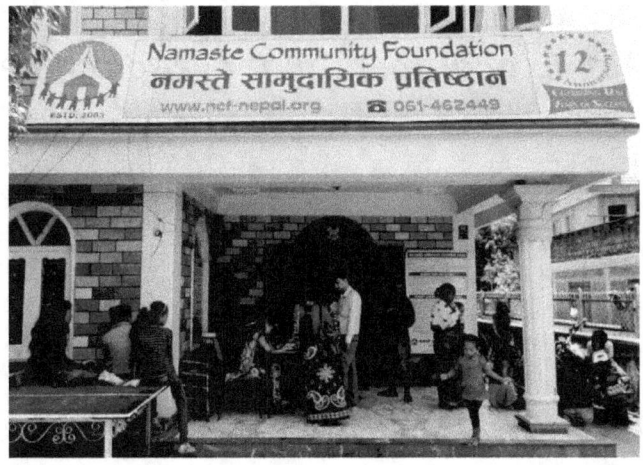

small Himalayan villages, in the churches and especially in an orphanage, Namaste Children's Home, that has been doing wonderful work for children and the community since 2003. With a broad base of help, Vicky initiated the placement of computers in the orphanage's library, improved the facilities, placed hundreds of books and developed an on-line reading program. The dynamic founder, Visma Paudel, inspired us to become part of the work from the moment we met him.

Also, Pastor Grishma of Nayagaun Church in Pokhara led us into works of faith in various surrounding locations. Trekking into the foothills to speak in small Christian gatherings with the help of an interpreter, Prakash, began to fulfill my

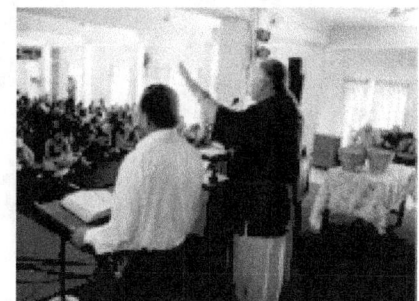

passion for reaching this region with the gospel of Jesus Christ. Our family and friends helped with the financial support of pastor's transportation providing a small motorcycle and other needs.

And, fresh in our heart, is a newly formed neighborhood kid's club called, "Team Orange." On our last visit I was able inspire some school aged children to clean the area of paper/plastic trash and reward them with fresh oranges, hot vegetable soup and volleyball games. They are eager 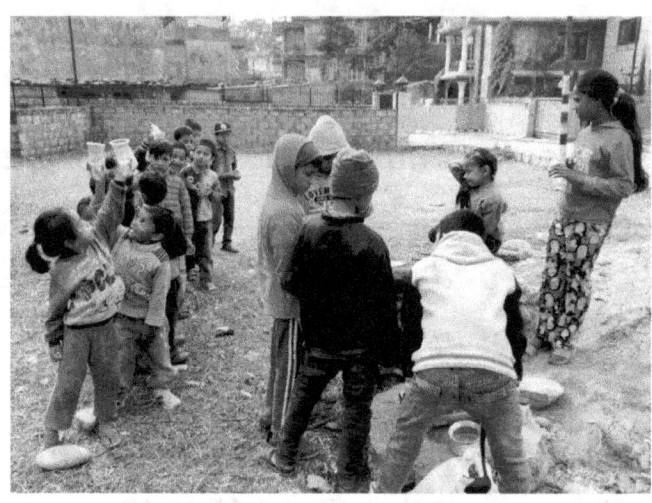 *to continue once we return to our Airbnb apartment that overlooks the village, near to all of our work.*

We now live most of the year in Cotacachi, Ecuador where we are involved with the needy in a village where we can live on our modest pension, write and self-publish, teach, love our new South American neighbors and look to return to Nepal, once a year, on another mission trip to Pokhara. Royalties from our books help us along the way.

Thanks so much... Kenny and Vicky Allen

About Nepal...

Words fall short of effectively describing this land of 30 million people, home of 7 out of 10 of the tallest mountains in the world, located south of China and north of India. So, beyond words, I am pleased to offer some of my photographs to introduce you to a region that is a one-hour flight west of Kathmandu, or a seven-hour bus ride, should you want a twisting and turning ground level view through the Himalayan foothills. The town we know best is Pokhara and is located primarily on the southern shore of Lake Fewa, beyond which are the Himalayan foothills that rapidly ascend to the Annapurna Range, peaking at over 24,000 feet.

Average per capita income in Nepal is $2.00 per day, making it one of the poorest countries in the world. Recently, in April of 2015, a massive, devastating earthquake rippled eastward from near Pokhara all the way to Kathmandu and beyond. Thousands of lives were lost, tens of thousands of homes were destroyed and hundreds of thousands were affected economically since tourism, which is their main source of national income, plunged to dismal levels and political upheaval closed the southern border, into and out of India.

Yet, our visits afforded us the opportunity of seeing the resiliency of the people as they adapted to the situations. We believe that you will see a measure of character in their faces, their efforts, their core family values, their common concern for one another and an up and coming, more enlightened youth. Most remarkable is the fact that Christianity is becoming a dynamic force in this once official Hindu nation that now has a new constitution in place which should stimulate progress in many ways. Doors are open more than ever to proclaim Christ where once there seemed no way without intense persecution and even imprisonment.

There seems to be a new day dawning in Nepal and it is a land where so little is able to go so far, if placed in the right hands. We hope this book awakens you to the needs of the poor, not just in Nepal, but elsewhere around the globe and that acts of yours prompted by faith will arise from within you heart.

Two Sections of This Book

The first half... *is for viewing my black and white photographs and reading about the particulars of the setting.*

The second half... *is for coloring, adding your touch as a means of engaging with the needs of these resilient Nepali people.*

Added step... *after coloring, If you desire, you can take a photo of your work and send it as an attachment to* <u>coffeetablecoloringbook@gmail.com</u>.

Upon receiving, Vicky and I will choose some of the choice, creative, works and post them on an art page of my website for others to view at <u>www.kennyreeseallen.com</u>, at the coloring book page. If you like, you can write your first name, your city and state and even your age. After receiving your art work, we will send you a digital certificate of achievement, especially intended for encouraging the young, school-aged artist who has shown an interest in art and the helping the poor.

PLEASE REMEMBER THAT THE FIRST HALF OF THIS BOOK IS FOR VIEWING AND THE SECOND HALF, BEGINNING ON PAGE 81, IS FOR COLORING ONLY WITH THE PERMISSION OF THE OWNER.

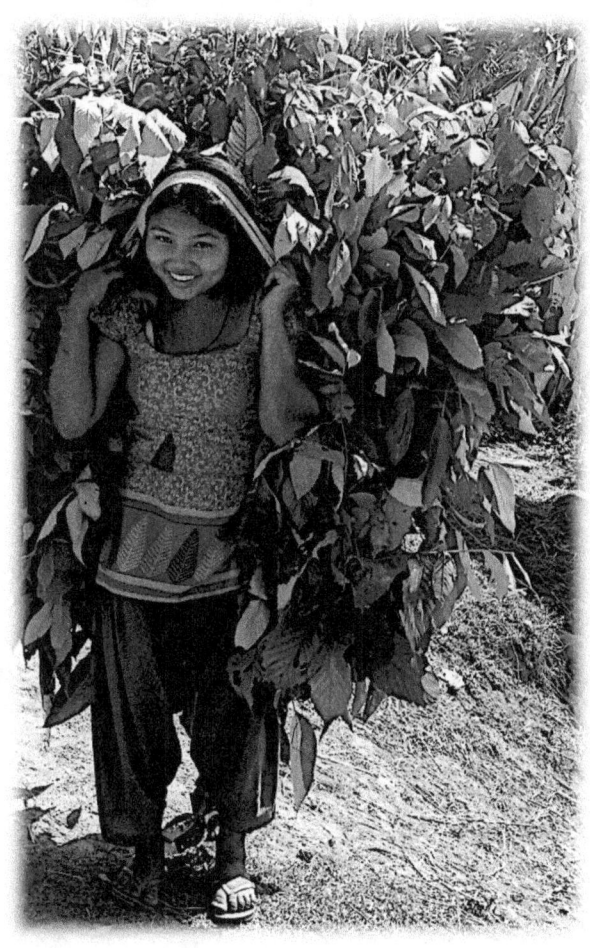

A young woman from a small Himalayan village brings a full load of freshly chopped verdant branches and leaves on her back to help feed the livestock. Women of all ages often carry the equivalent of their body weight on their shoulders for miles, making several trips each day in and out of the valley below to insure that needs are met.

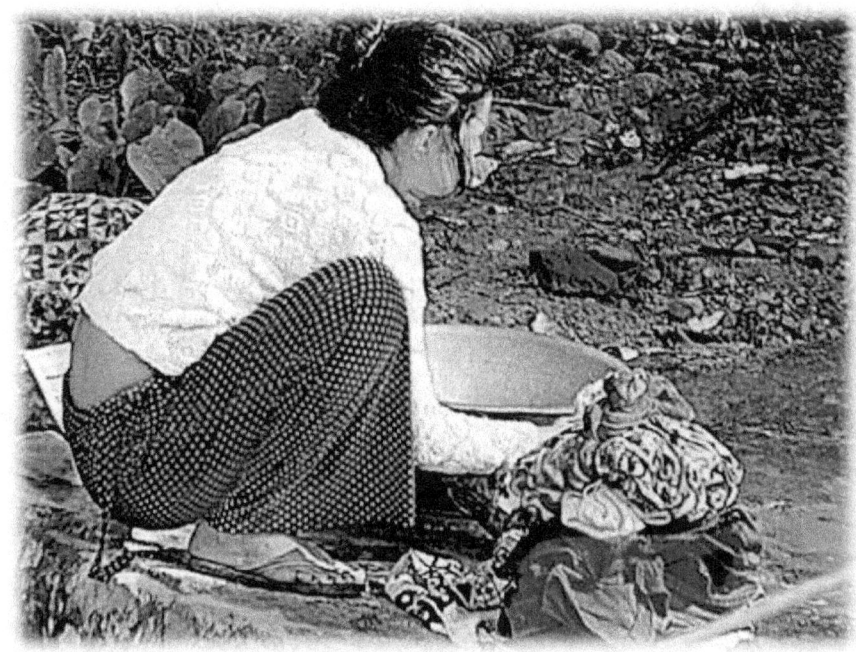

Outside the kitchen window of our third floor apartment in Pokhara, throughout the day, you can observe women and children utilizing the fresh water that flows from the Himalayan streams and converges into a low-lying area used to wash clothes and sponge bathe. The cold weather does not deter them, nor does the lack of soap as they scrub their colorful fabrics against each other and the smooth rocks until clean.

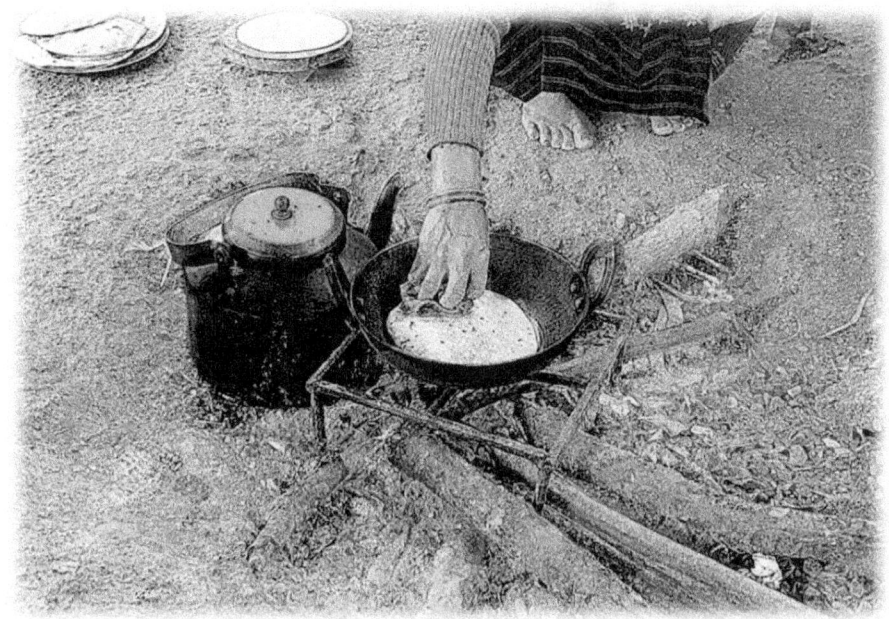

A Nepali Christian woman kneels barefooted before an open fire on a chilly Sunday morning as she hand-kneads dough and cooks bread for dozens of villagers who have gathered for discipleship classes and a church worship service in the Himalayan foothills. Always nearby are helpful teenagers who sit in a circle to cut vegetables for the lunchtime meal. Also, other adults work in the crude kitchen area and prepare soup in twenty-gallon steel containers to be cooked later over a wood-fired grill since propane is sparse and expensive.

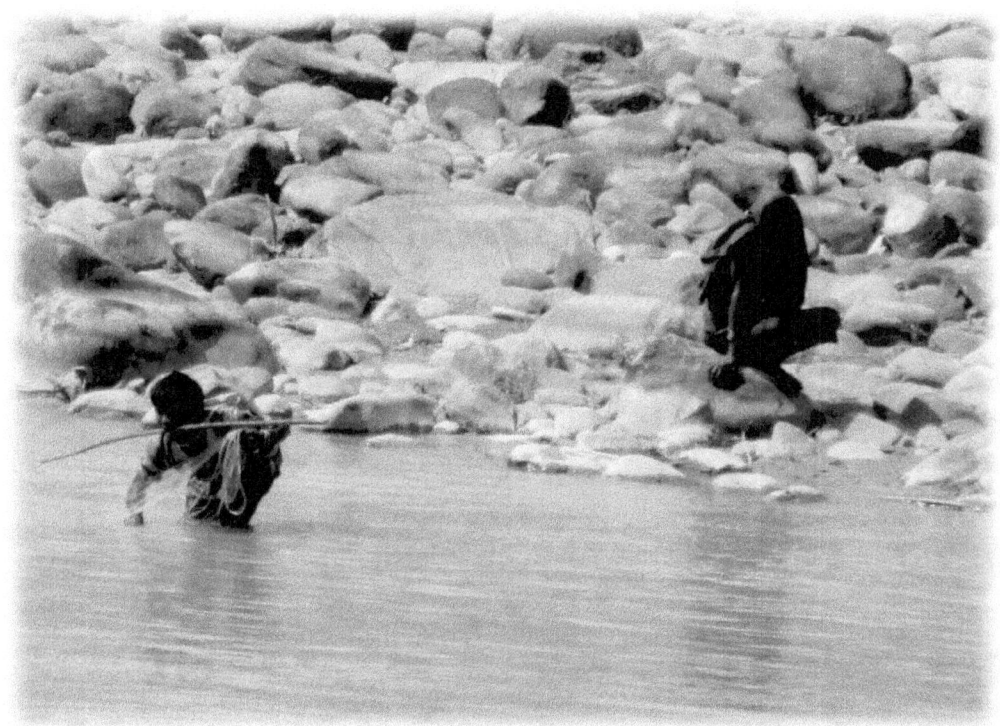

A young man "hunts for fish" in an icy river that swiftly flows out of the Himalaya Mountains early each Spring. He is carrying a spear in his mouth and has a large casting net over his shoulder He has a determined expression on his face as his friend watches and waits for his conquest. The fish are very small, taking perhaps as many as 20 to feed one adult and they cook them whole, head and all, for their late evening feasts.

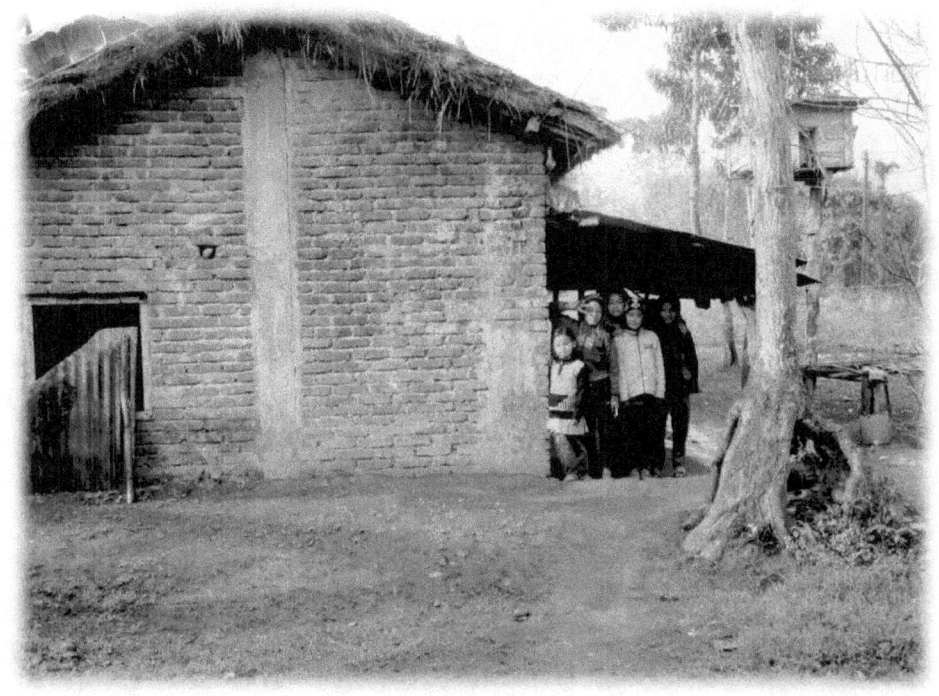

These children are among thousands in Nepal who were rescued from the earthquake of 2015 that decimated hundreds of villages in the foothills and thousands of buildings in Kathmandu. Unknown numbers were killed and many remain homeless to this day. In this case above, some kind and generous Nepali people near the southern border, just north of India, took these children and their mother and father into their care, bought them clothing, backpacks, books, provided education, food, etc., and they now live safely in this rustic building with a thatched roof in the back of this one family's home. These children are profoundly poor yet kind and respectful and do much of the caring for the animals and the gardens.

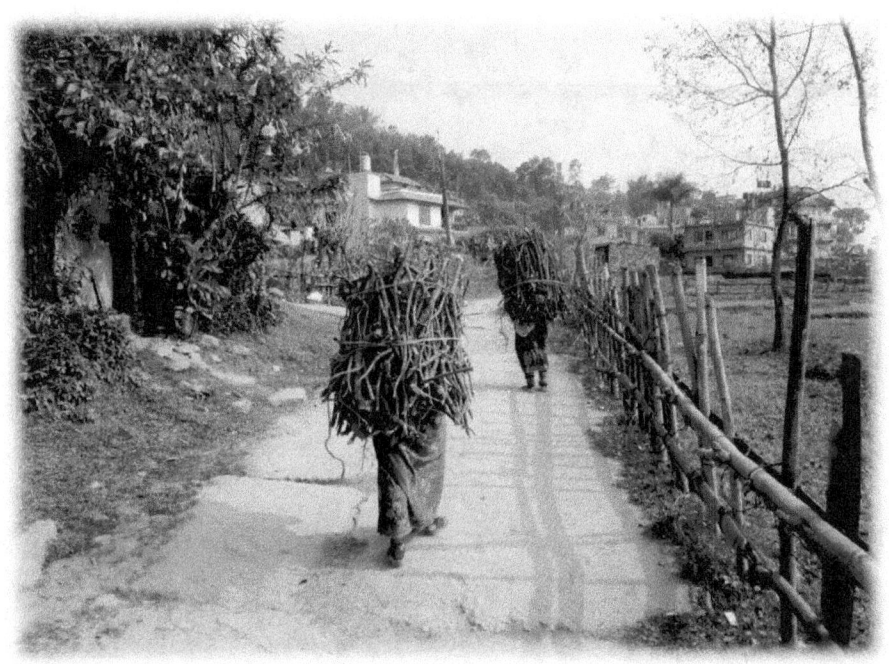

These two are carrying a load of firewood that they harvested from distant hillsides in order to provide their families with fuel for cooking and for heating their small homes. This is within a few meters of our apartment where we stay on our visits to Pokhara, hopefully we will return once each year. There was a propane shortage the last time we were there due to a blockade at the India border due to resistance to the new constitution. These Nepali people are adaptable and find ways to survive through hard work and strong family ties.

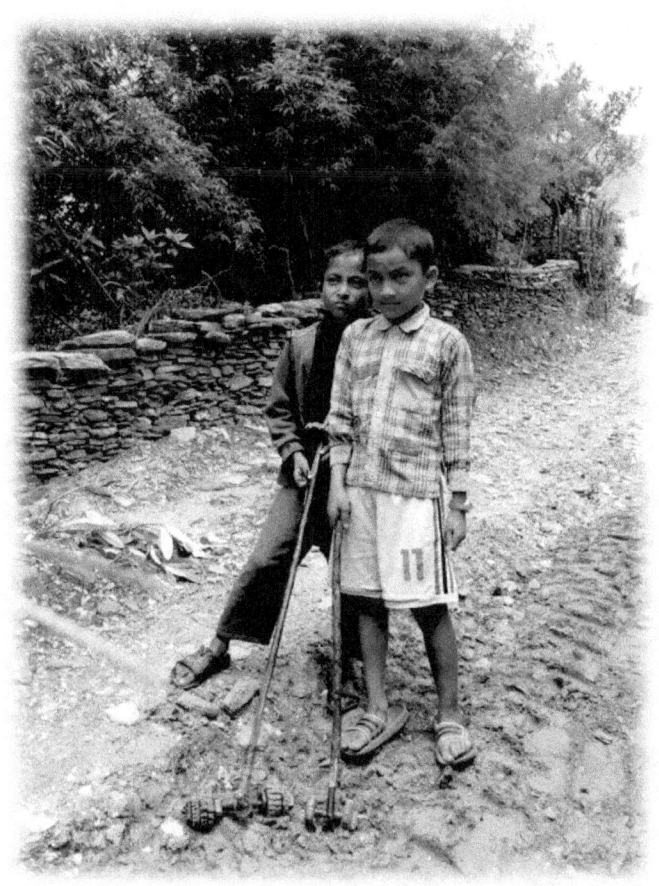

We came across these two young men as we trekked near Dhampus Village, Nepal, a day's walk north of Pokhara at an elevation of over 6,000 feet. These "stick and wheels" toys were manufactured by a family member using throw-away flip-flop rubber pieces of shoes for their wheels, a straight branch, a nail for a swivel and a carved, round piece of wood for a steering wheel. They race up and down the paths and need nothing but these to entertain themselves for hours.

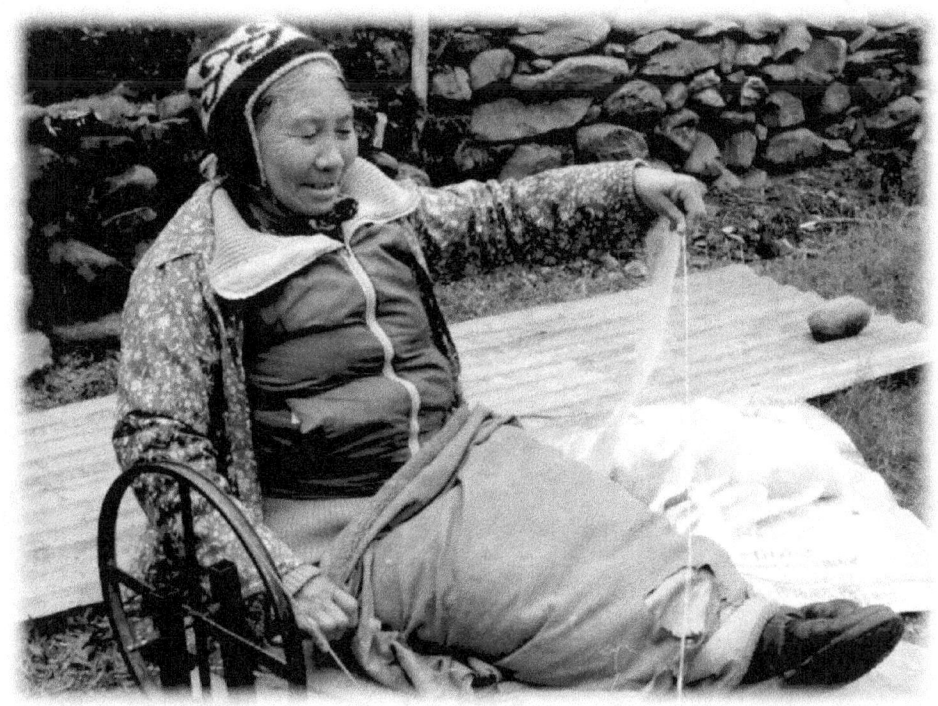

Some years back I met a young Tibetan woman with three of her friends who were selling souvenirs in Dhampus Village. On our next visit she introduced us to her mother who lives in a settlement that is a one-hour bus ride from Pokhara. This industrious woman, nearly ninety years old, spins cotton into yarn for hours each day, maintains a vegetable garden from which she harvests a crop in order to carry to the closest highway about three miles away where she sells at her roadside stand and also cares for her ailing and aged husband. She was a joy to be near.

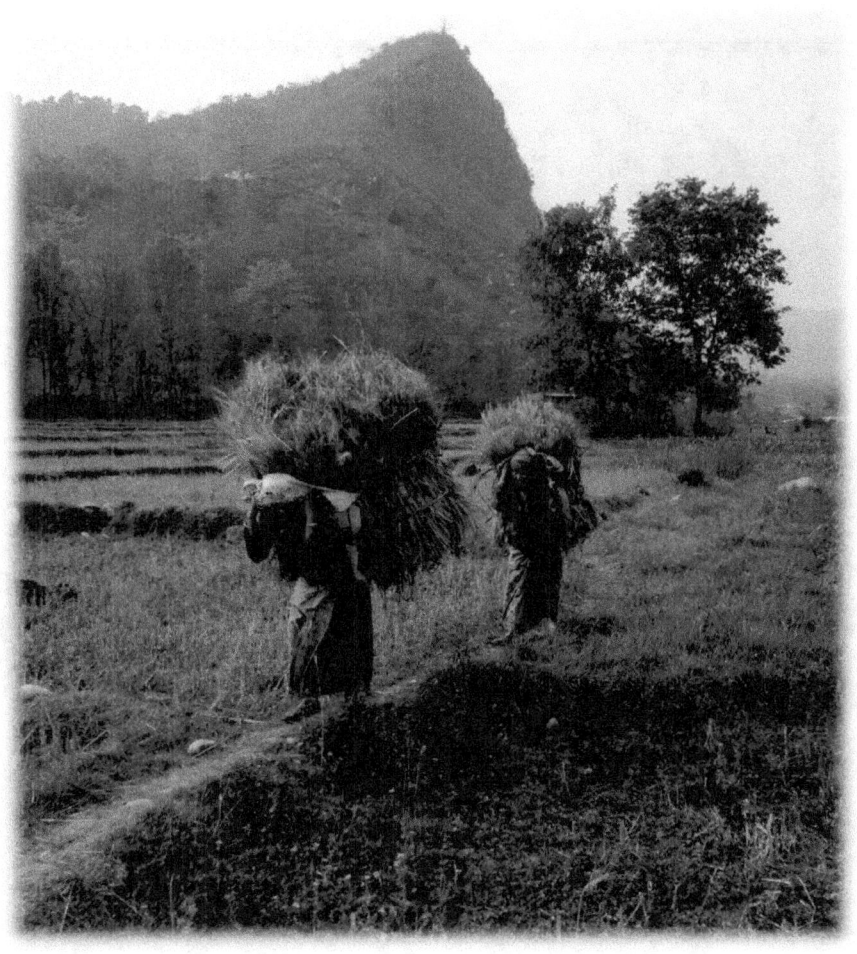

Many small villages have cattle to feed from which they sustain an income as they market milk and beef to others and have food for themselves. These two women, like so many others, march in and out of the hills many times each day with the necessary straw on their backs which they hand-harvest, sun-up to sundown.

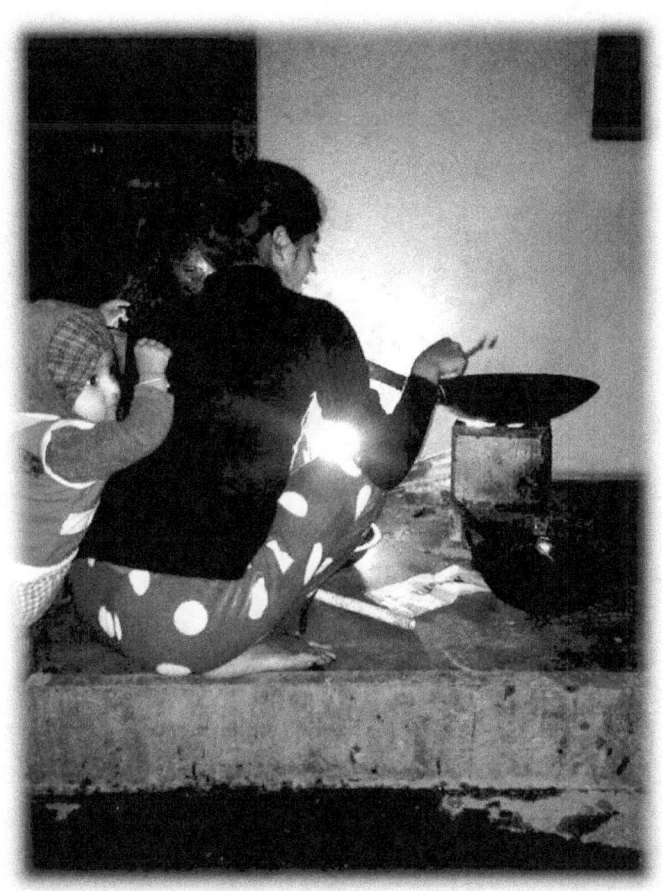

We had not lived long in Nepal before we were invited to a gathering of neighbors just below our apartment where a young woman graciously prepared a wonderful meal for us. She cooked outdoors, as usual, while caring for a family member's young child. The evening meal was delicious and this image brings fond memories of the hospitality and kindness of the Nepali people.

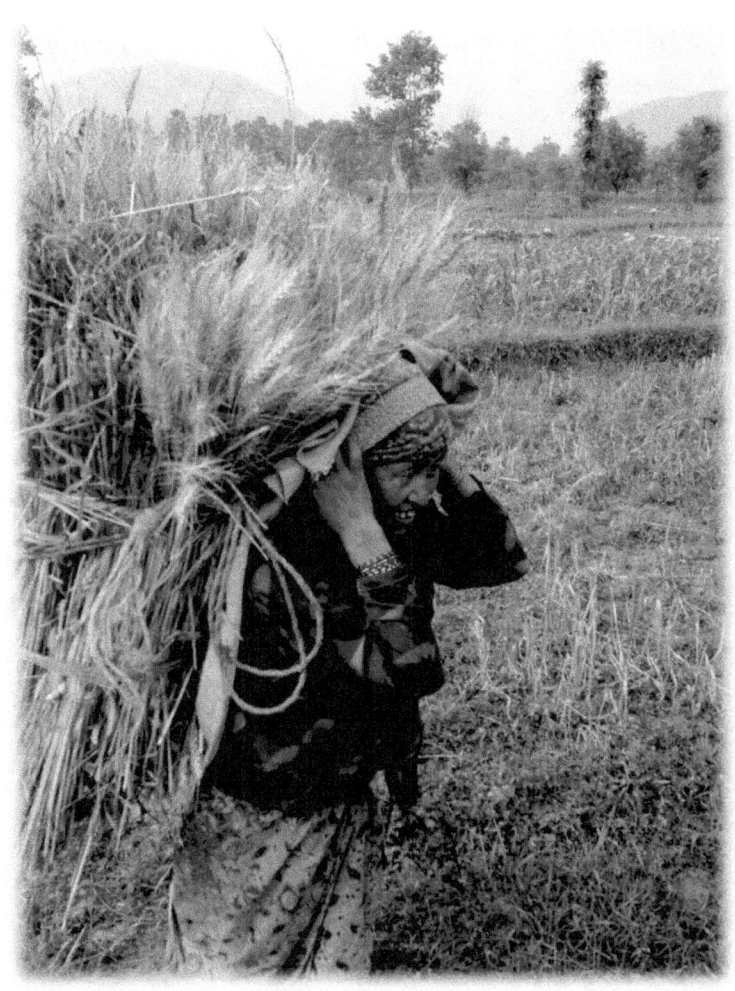

You saw the two women carrying straw out of the hills from a previous photo and this is a close-up of one of the women as she passes by, joyfully bearing a heavy load for others.

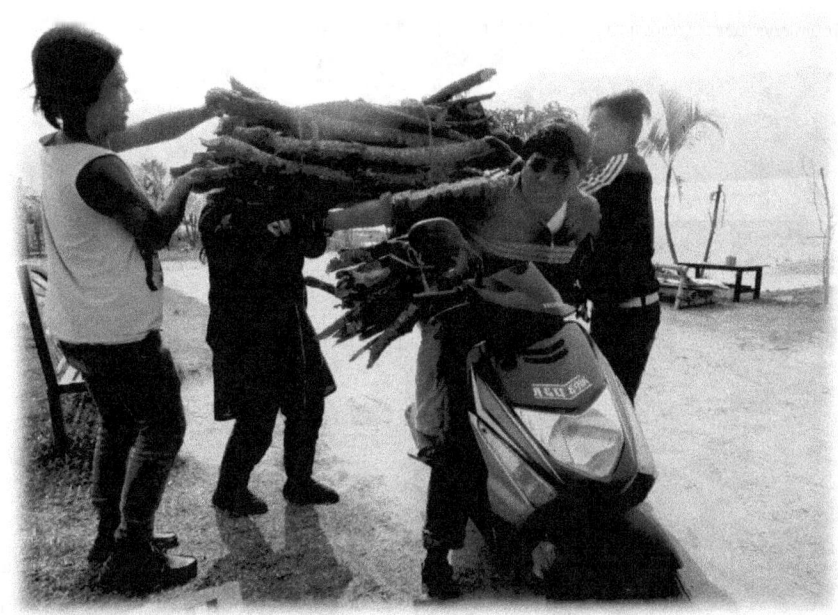

While sitting on a bench that overlooks Lake Fewa in Pokhara, I witnessed the cooperative spirit of four young men who were loading firewood onto the back of a motorcycle for delivery to family and neighbors during the fuel shortage. All vehicles are incredibly expensive due to burdensome taxation. In some cases, import fees can be as high as 100 percent. Fuel is scarce and long lines at the pumps are the norm for taxi drivers and motorcyclists.

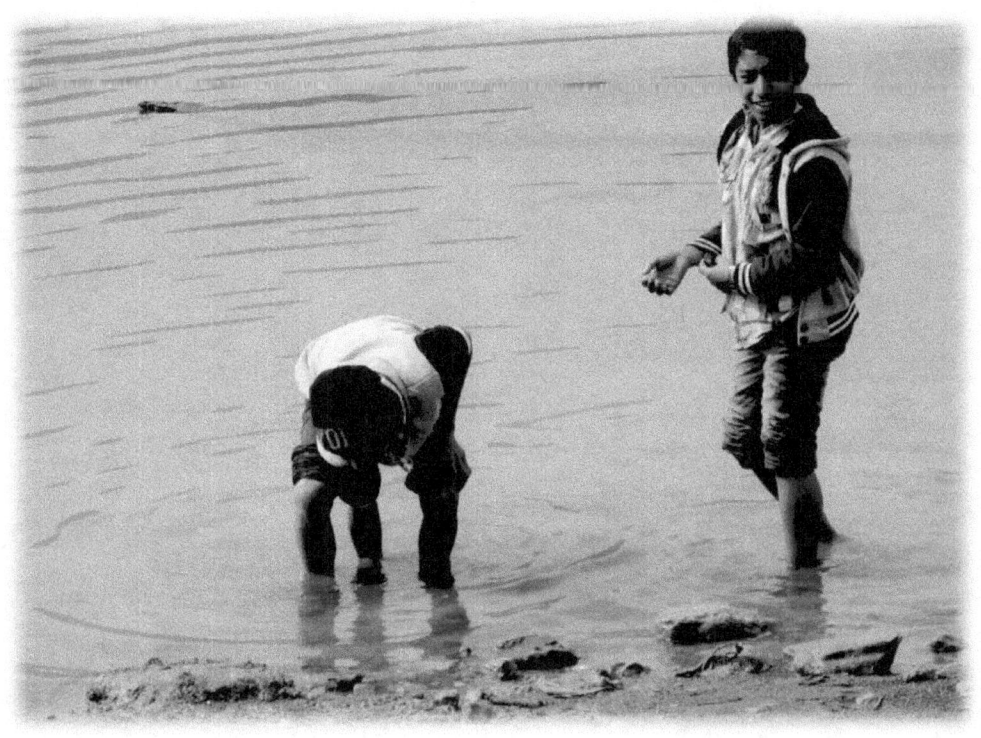

Team Orange had set up a portable gas cooker near the edge of Lake Fewa and these two young men decided they could add to the meal by pulling some mollusks out of the muddy shoreline. They brought them to the waiting kids and then boiled them, cracked them open and many enjoyed them as a delicious delicacy. It was when these two young men did something for the well-being of others that you could sense a spring in their step and a glow in their countenance.

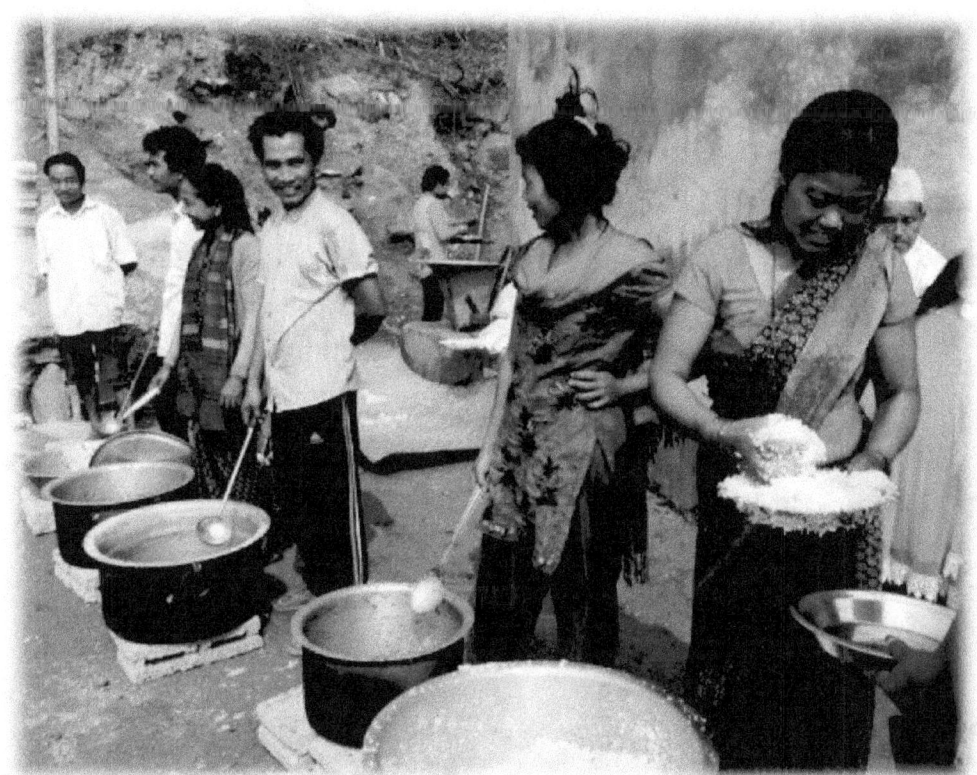

Finally, after years and months of intensive labor that had to be added to their daily chores in their village, these faithful served up for the entire community a meal just outside of their renovated church building. An earthquake had rendered their place of worship unsafe for their regular Christian services. Yet, on this day, they rejoiced and celebrated the fruit of their labor which provided a greater opportunity for others to visit and hear the good news of Jesus Christ.

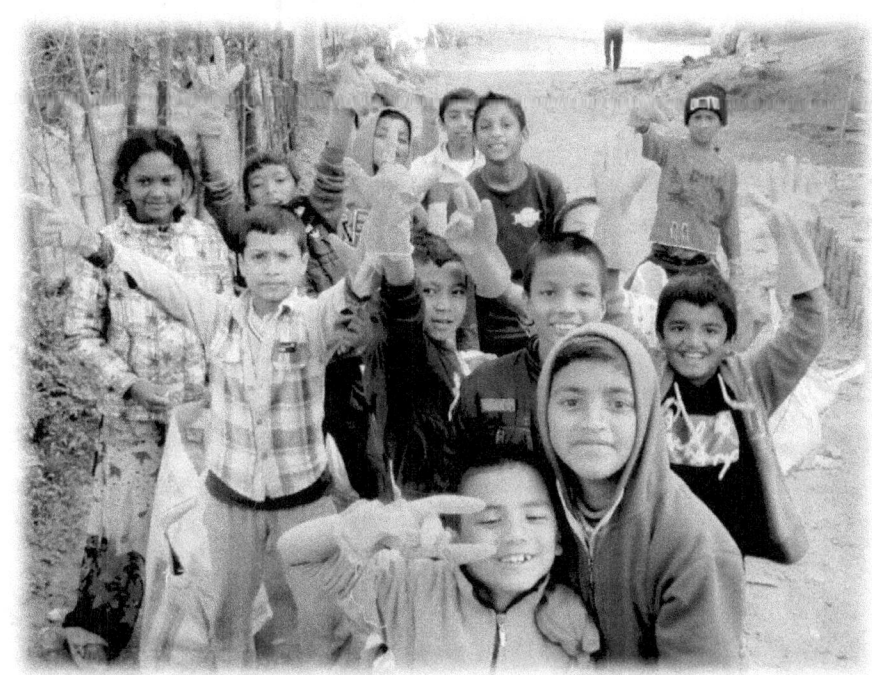

Most of the parents of these kids were not pleased that their children had relegated themselves to picking up trash in the neighborhood in their Team Orange endeavors. Yet, as the area began to reflect an increased measure of cleanliness, other workers wanted to join in as they saw how they could be used, not to mention that as a reward they would be given fresh oranges, hot soup and the equipment needed to play a supervised game of volleyball. Parents became proud. Go Team Orange!

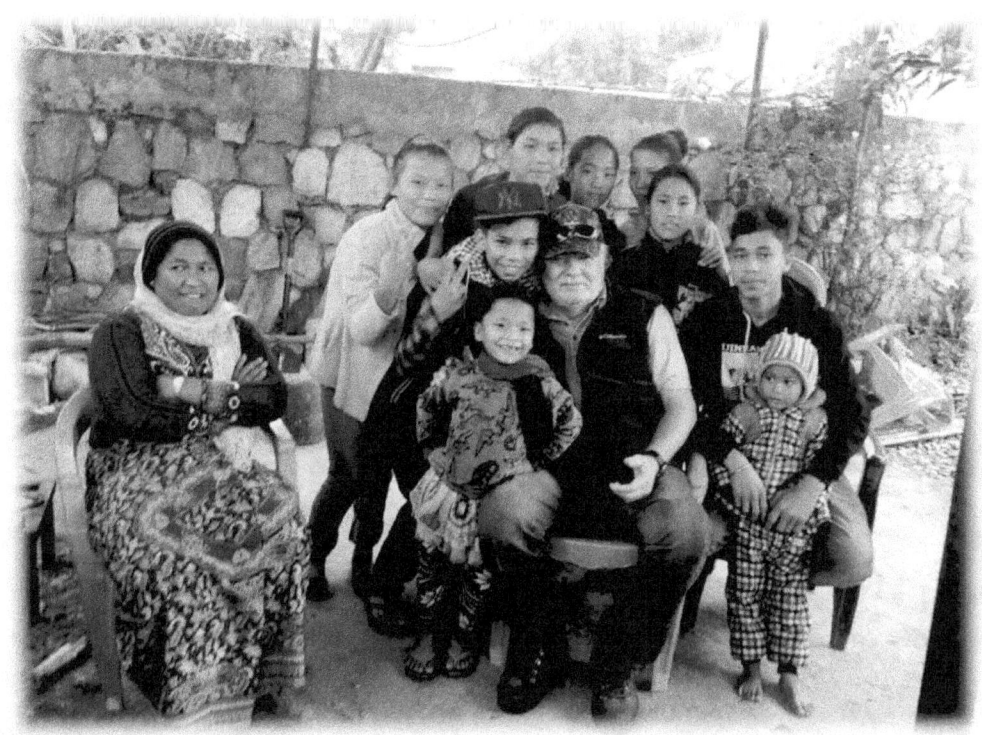

These are just a few of the dozens of young people who came to a weekday church meeting in their village south of Pokhara, Nepal. They wanted to be taught, as we say, "discipled", as to how best to follow Christ and share their Christian faith with their friends. Distinct in this culture is parental oversight as you can see from one of the mothers being close by.

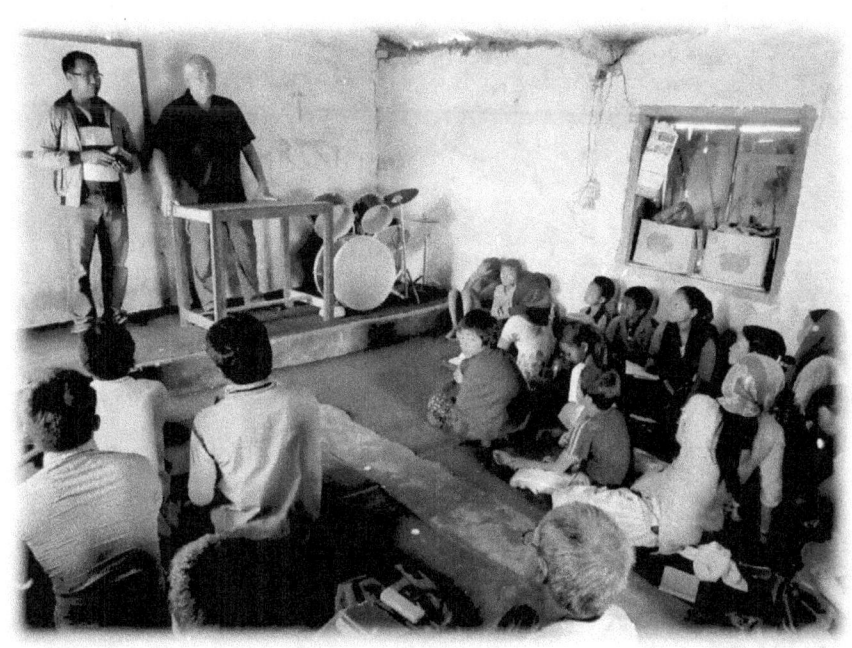

After two hours of riding in an overcrowded van, we turned off the main highway and weaved our way up a one lane blacktop into a quaint village. From there we walked for two hours into the heart of a steep walled valley that isolated this un-incorporated region of farmers. This was on a weekday and many had to remain in the fields, working, but several attended a Christian teaching and a worship service. Weeks after this photo, the building was severely damaged by an earthquake and yet they were able to rebuild it with help from other churches in the region and financial assistance from abroad.

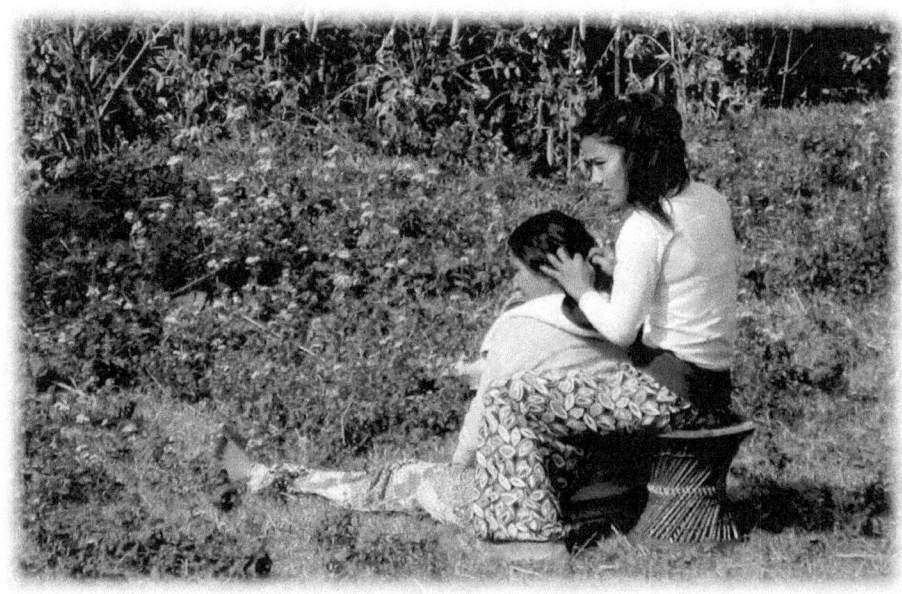

Just off of the third-floor balcony of our apartment in Pokhara, only a few paces away, there is a flower enhanced field near a buffalo farm where this makeshift hair salon was set up. The one lady sat on her stool for about an hour and gently combed and braided her friend's hair. The women take pride in their colorful hand made garments, and love their long, beautifully flowing dark hair.

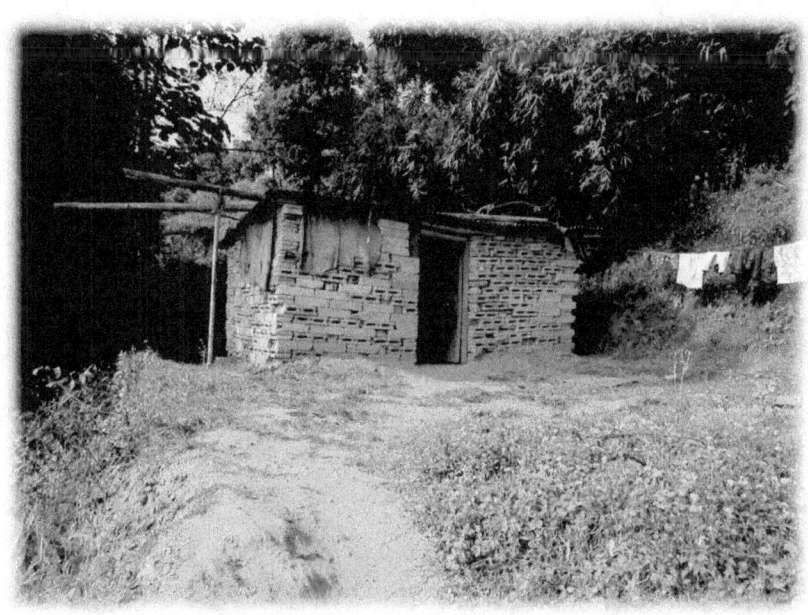

Trekking up into the foothills near our apartment, there appears this tiny home that was constructed from un-mortared concrete blocks with a tin roof, fitting for a family of four. The grounds were well-kept, the brightly colored clothes hanging on the line were fresh and clean and the woman working behind the home, was cordial as I passed by. I believe that if I had been with my wife, she would have invited us in for some ever present, always brewing, Nepali tea, deliciously unique to this land.

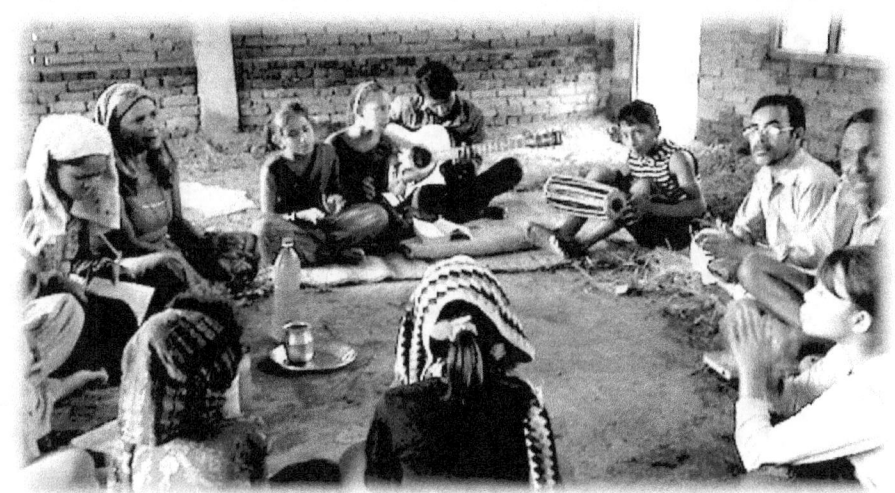

This unfinished church building provided no excuse for these faithful Christians to gather, even if it meant sitting on blankets on a dirt floor. Upon arrival, they offered us some warm buffalo milk yogurt and it was quite good. On the silver plate you can see the elements for the Lord's Supper that we would soon partake. Bibles abounded, the hand clapping and singing were lively and some tunes could be linked to westernized Christian music such as, "This is the day the Lord has made, let us rejoice and be glad in it."

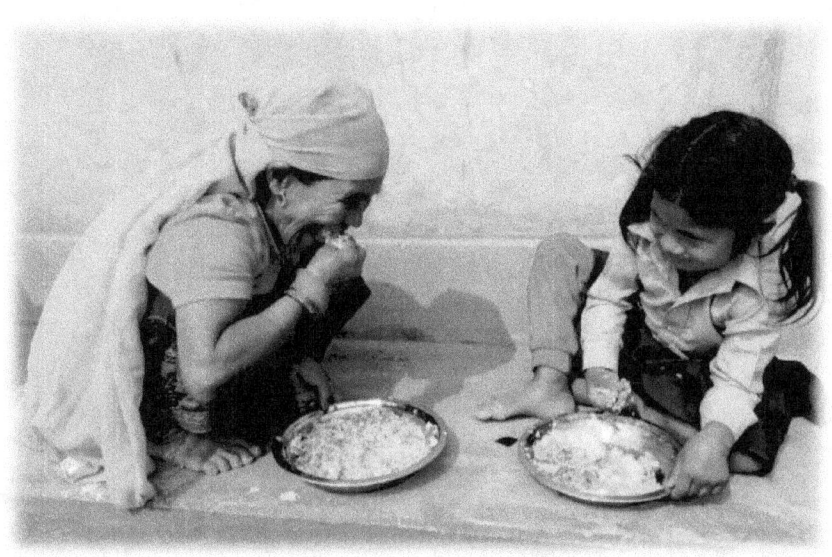

There is hardly ever any lasting separation of the old from the young, unless it is during school hours. Therefore, the children adapt their attitudes and respect more so to please their family elders rather than gaining unruliness from their peers. This older woman defies our flexibility standards by being able to squat for hours at a time, in the home, in the fields, or while eating with her granddaughter. They use no forks or spoons, only their hands for adeptly scooping in their meals.

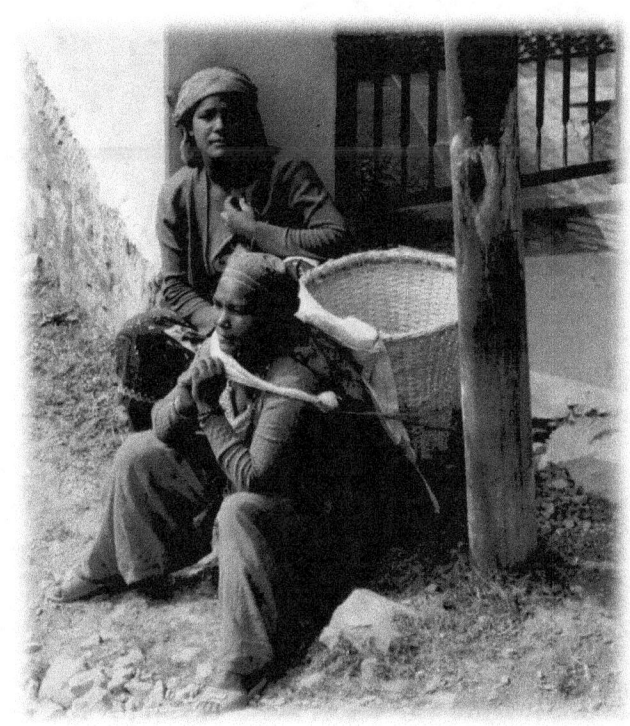

Without ever being able to verbally communicate in their language, I got in touch by way of mutual kindness and respect. These ladies had just come far down the foothills from a building site with their empty baskets that were once full of bricks. Anonymously leaving them a warm cup of soup, or an orange, or a sweet at their rest spot meant the world to them. I think they knew it was me, the long-haired American who watched from the balcony.

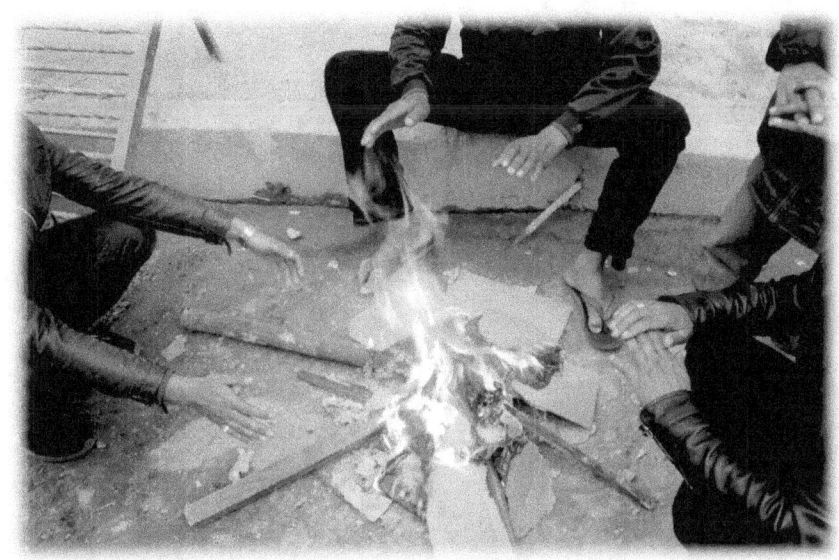

One cold month in particular, there was no propane due to a blockade at the Indian border. For warming their hands and feet at the curbside, these men built a fire from remnants of cardboard boxes and scrap pieces of wood. Luxuries for many of the profoundly poor include, shoes, hot water, food staples like rice and beans, a bed with a mattress and a roof over their heads. Many others circled these men, particularly the children in the village, in order to listen to the conversations of their elders and in order to stay warm.

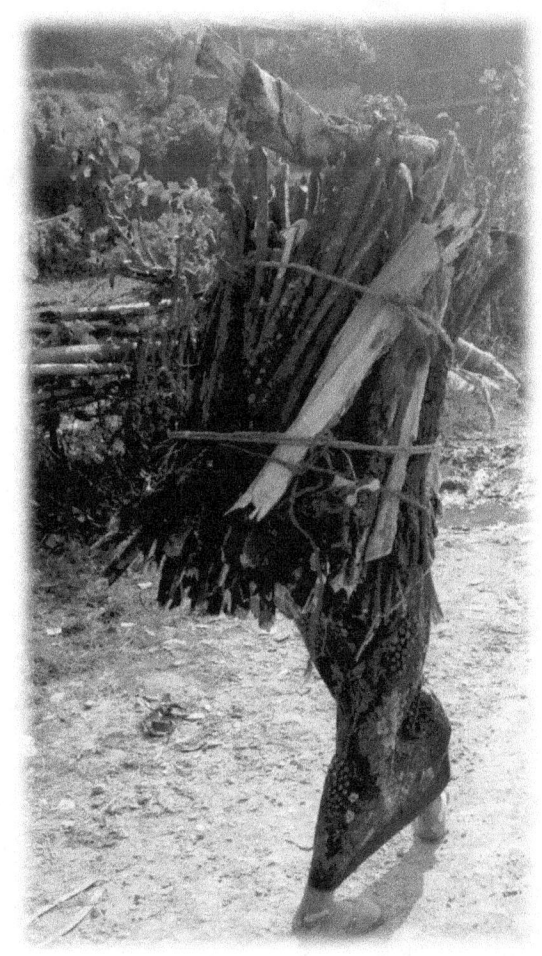

Here is a full load of firewood securely tied to the back of a woman who has carried 25 kilos of firewood, by foot, from the nearby hills. Often you see women in roles of rigorous manual labor, more so than men.

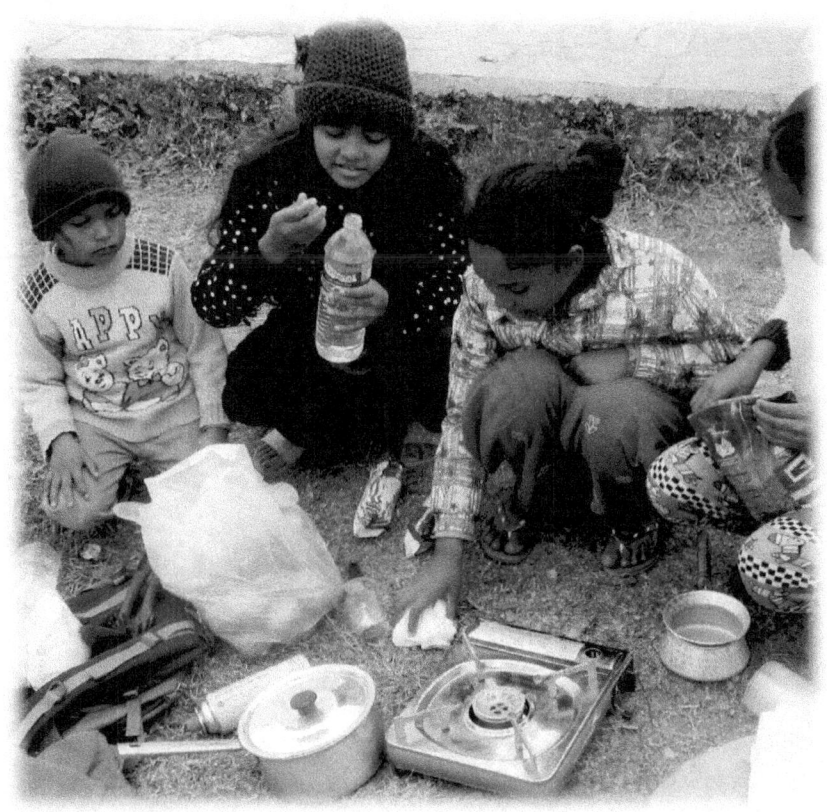

In a field near Lake Fewa, the ladies of Team Orange prepare soup for others, in particular for this young man who is drawn to the hope of an an orange and to the greater hope of a taste of vegetable soup. Many passersby had never seen a portable propane heater which we acquired for the team from a nearby city.

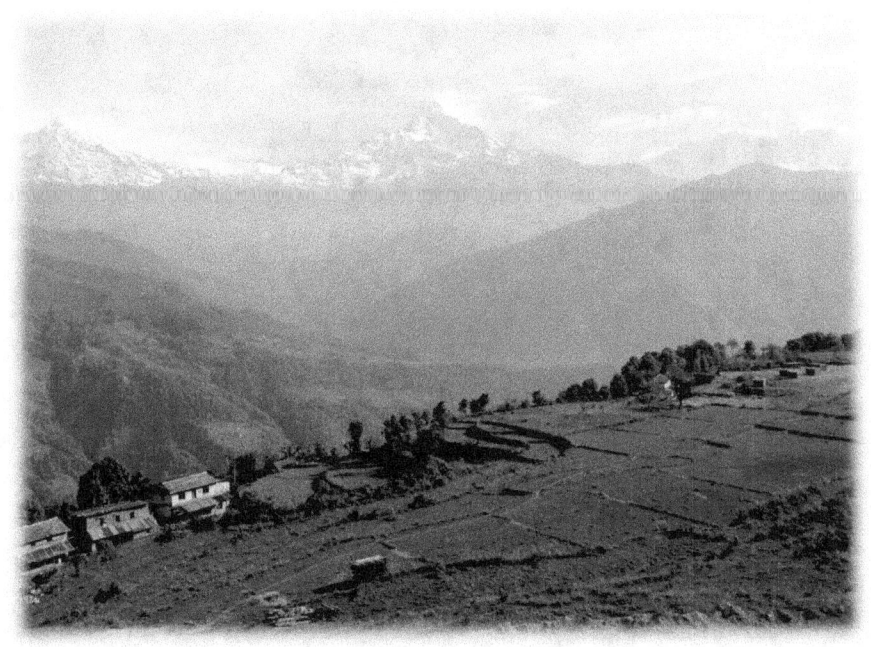

To the east of Dhampus Village, there lies this open field between farm houses that sits on the edge of a cavernous valley. This land was once available for purchase and development for such uses as; a Bed and Breakfast, a school, a medical clinic, a farm with small family dwellings, or a church. Actually, I believe, all of these could have worked on these 7 acres. This view, face on to the snow-capped Annapurna Range across the way about 40 miles, is magnificent and worth the strong consideration of revisiting with a plan for helping the villagers.

All coloring opportunities are here and beyond.

1)   Please do not color elsewhere outside of these 26 images beginning on page 81 that have been brightened, framed and texturized in the second half of the book.

2)   Please do not scribble but give it your best effort in order to maintain the integrity of the book for yourself and others.

3)   Please do not use any type of ink marker for it may bleed through the paper.

4)   Quality color pencils or crayons need to be used for best results. Take your time.

BONUS - If you like, you may photograph your work and send it to my email at <u>coffeetablecoloringbook@gmail.com</u> with your first name only and city and state, if you choose. If selected by my wife as excellent or exemplary, I will post it on my website and I will send you a digital certificate honoring your work.

Thank you for becoming more aware of the needy and I hope your compassion for the plight of poor has been heightened by your participation in reading and coloring this book. The purchase of this book helps us return to Nepal and you can order more from my website, at www.kennyreeseallen.com at the page that is entitled "Coloring Book." Go to the website to view those works that we selected for uploading. Thanks for participating. KRA

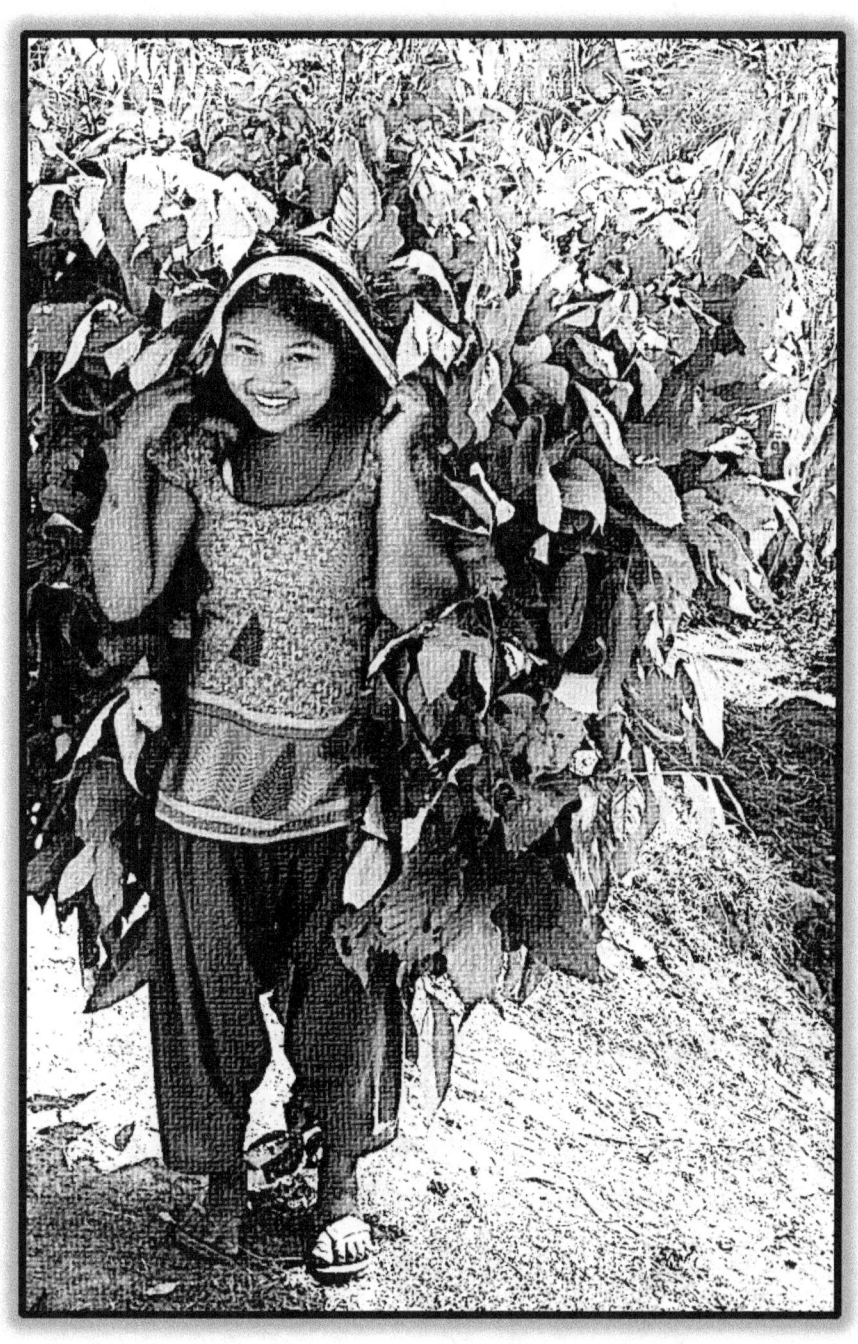

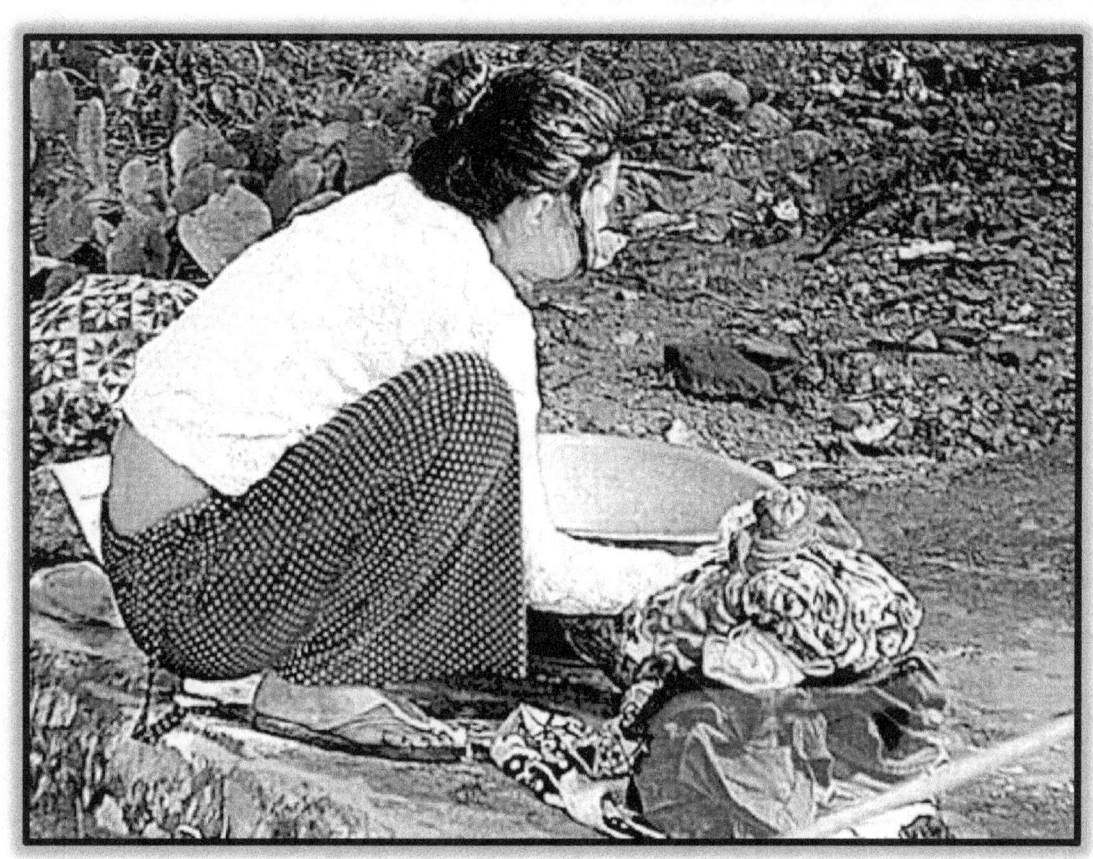

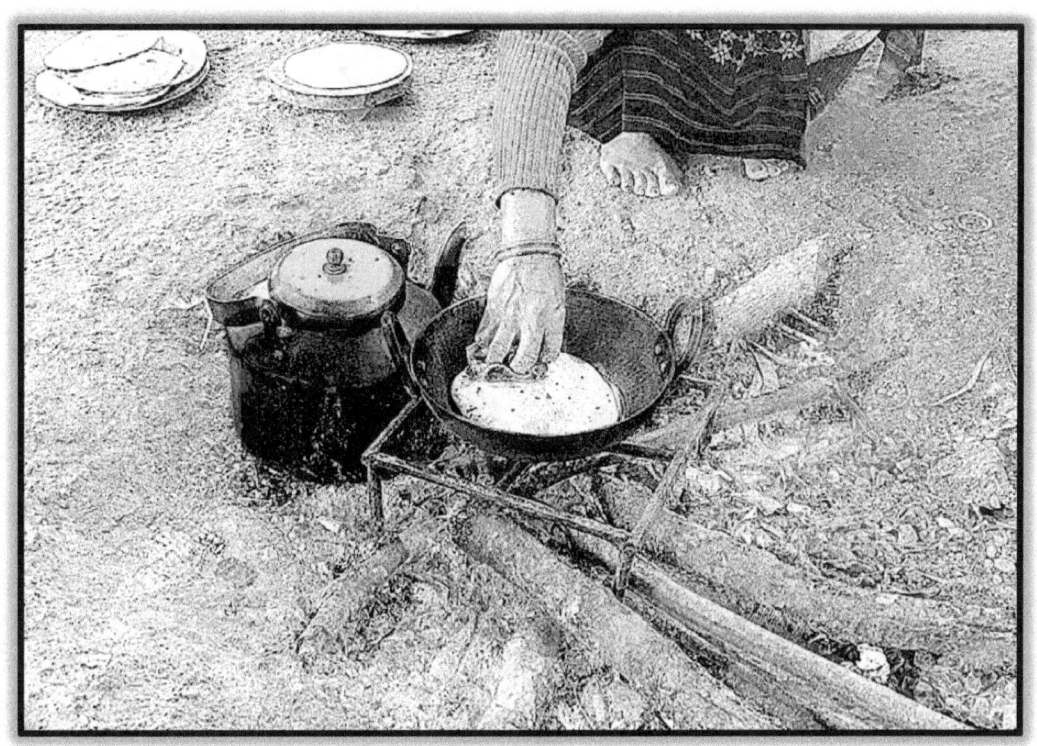

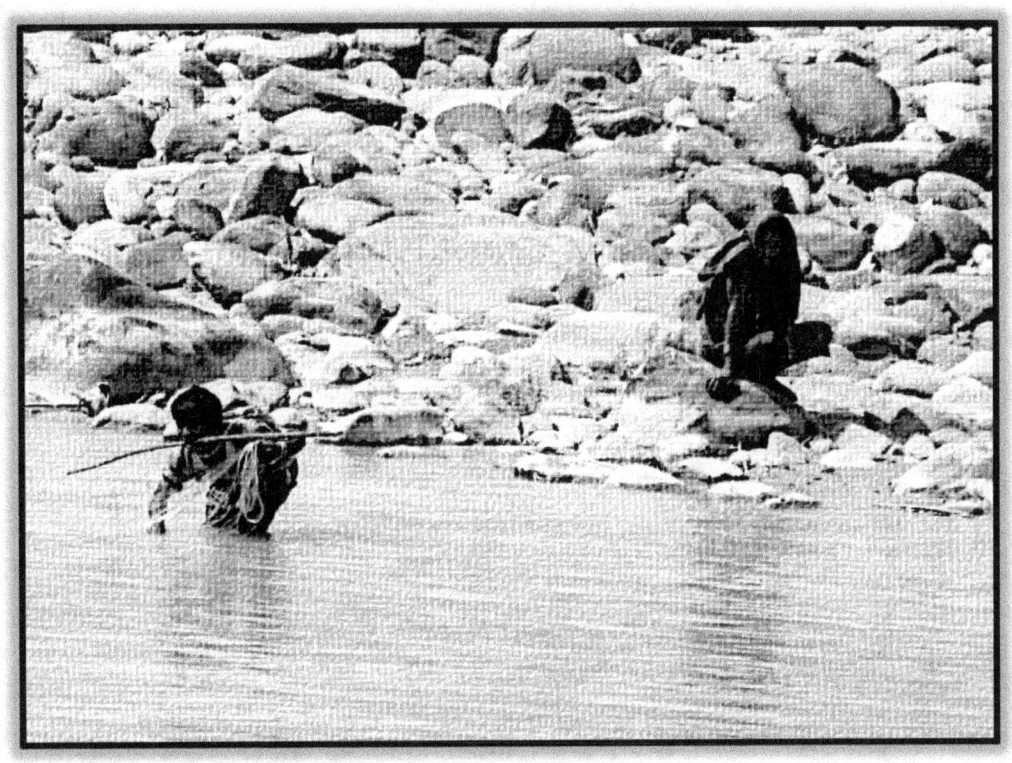

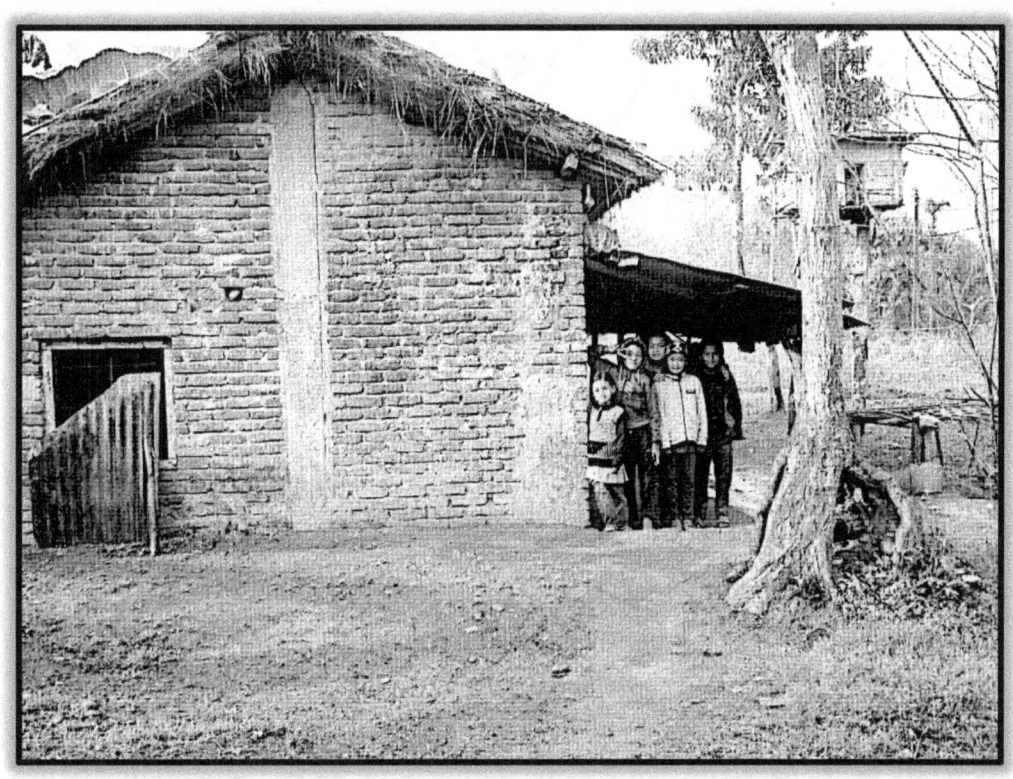

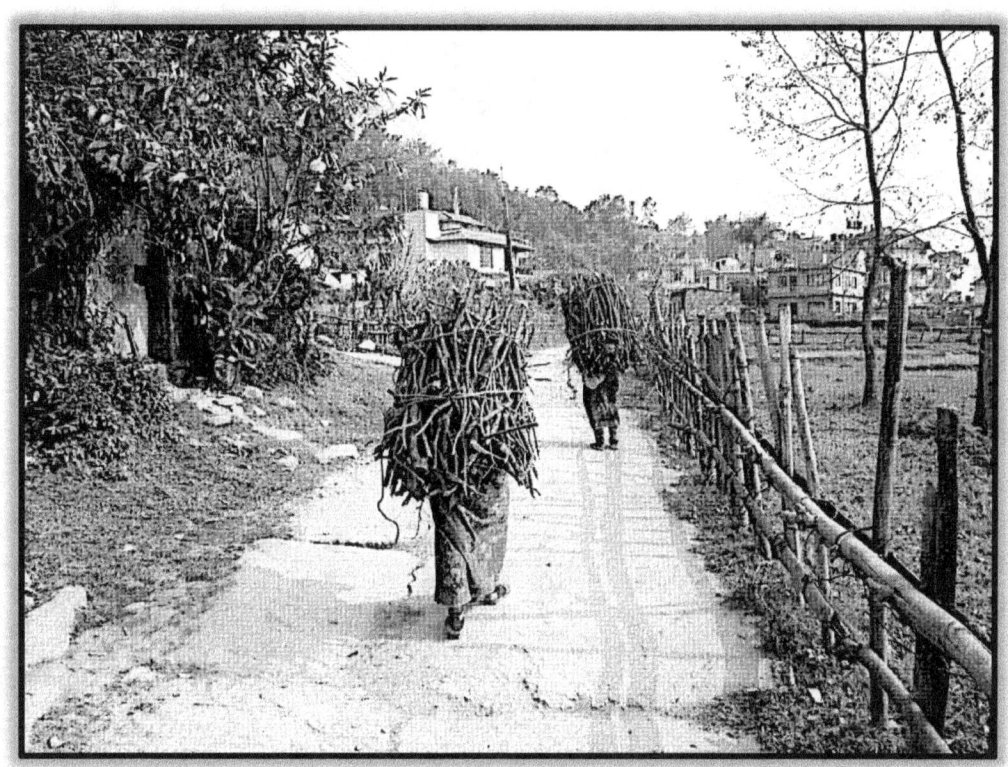

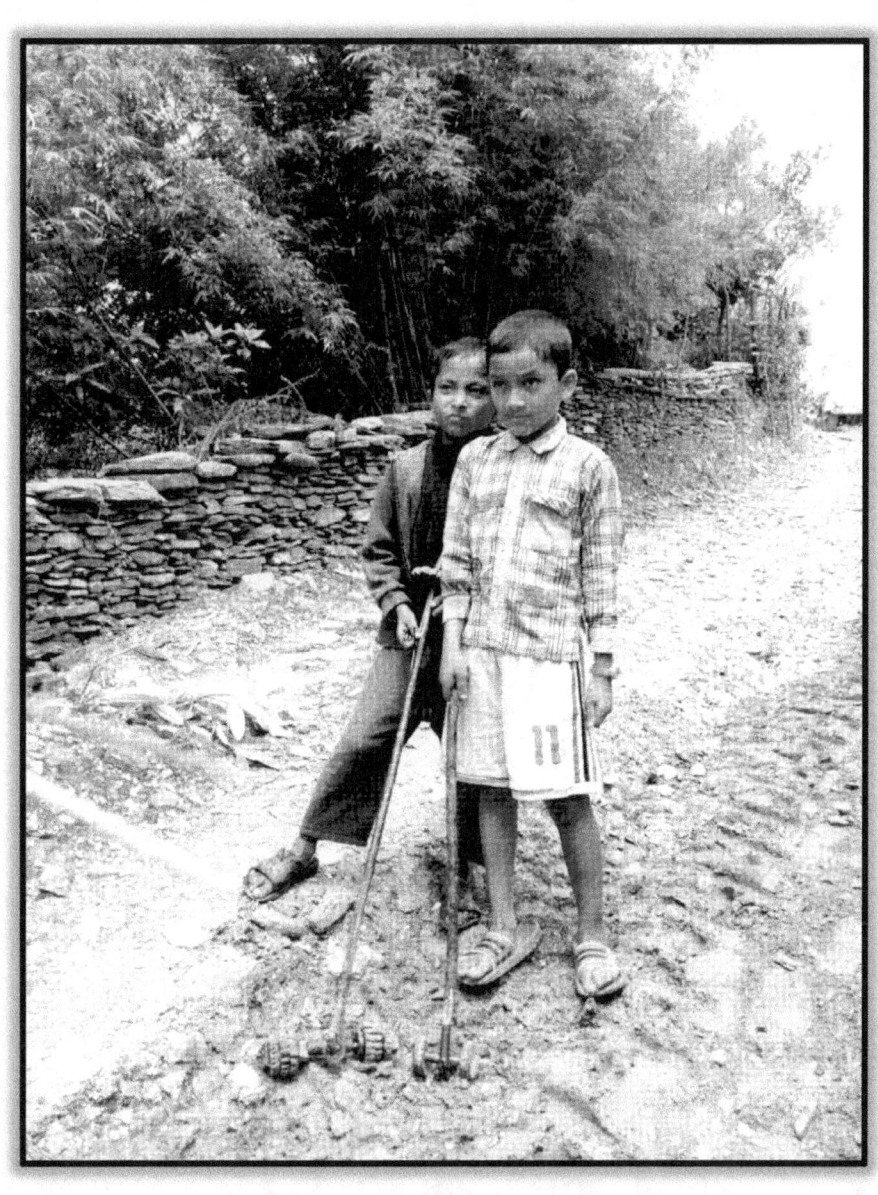

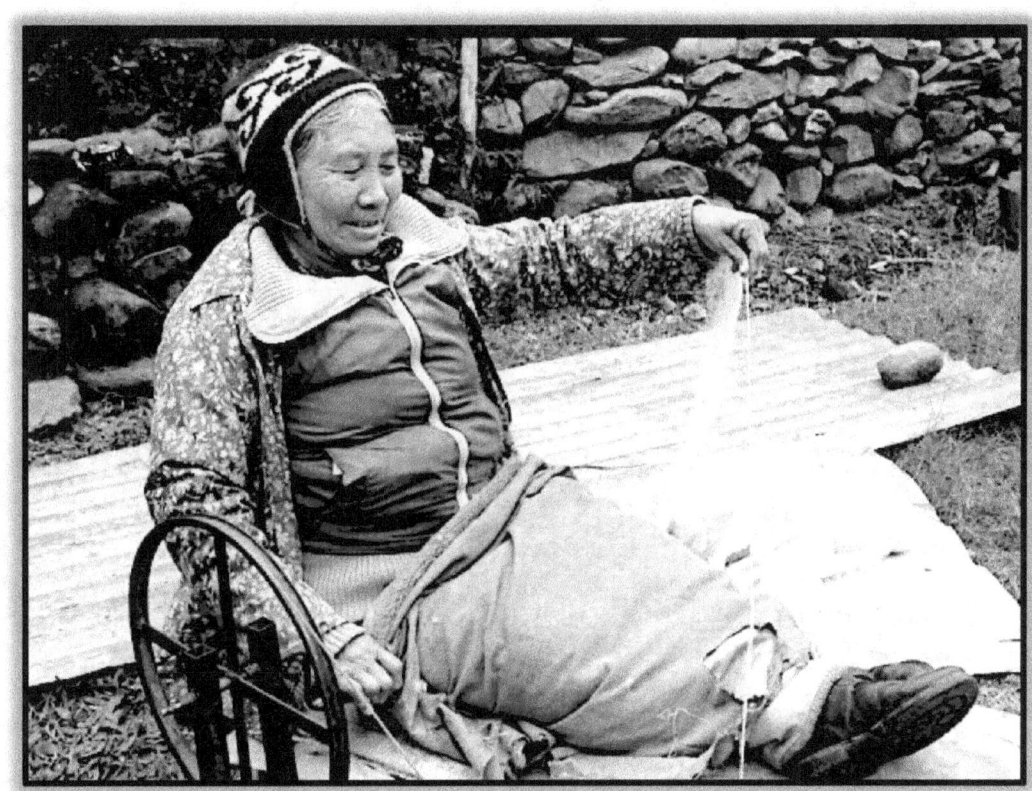

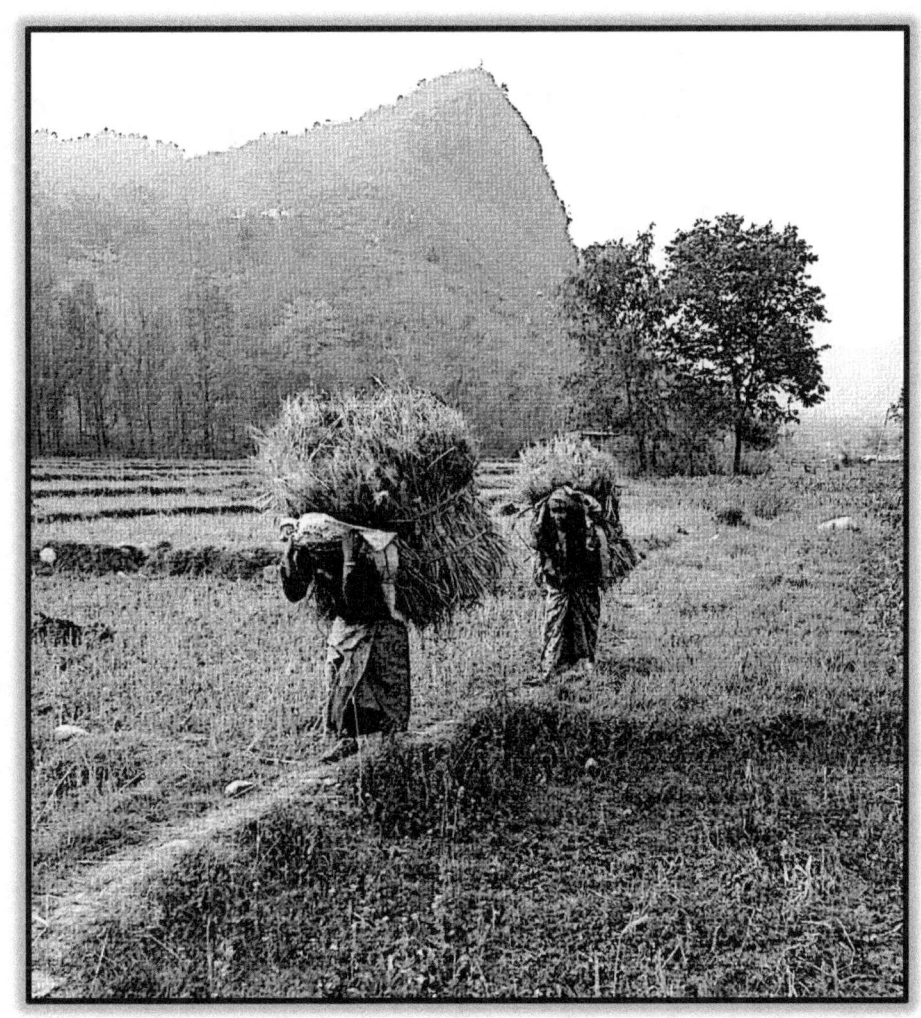

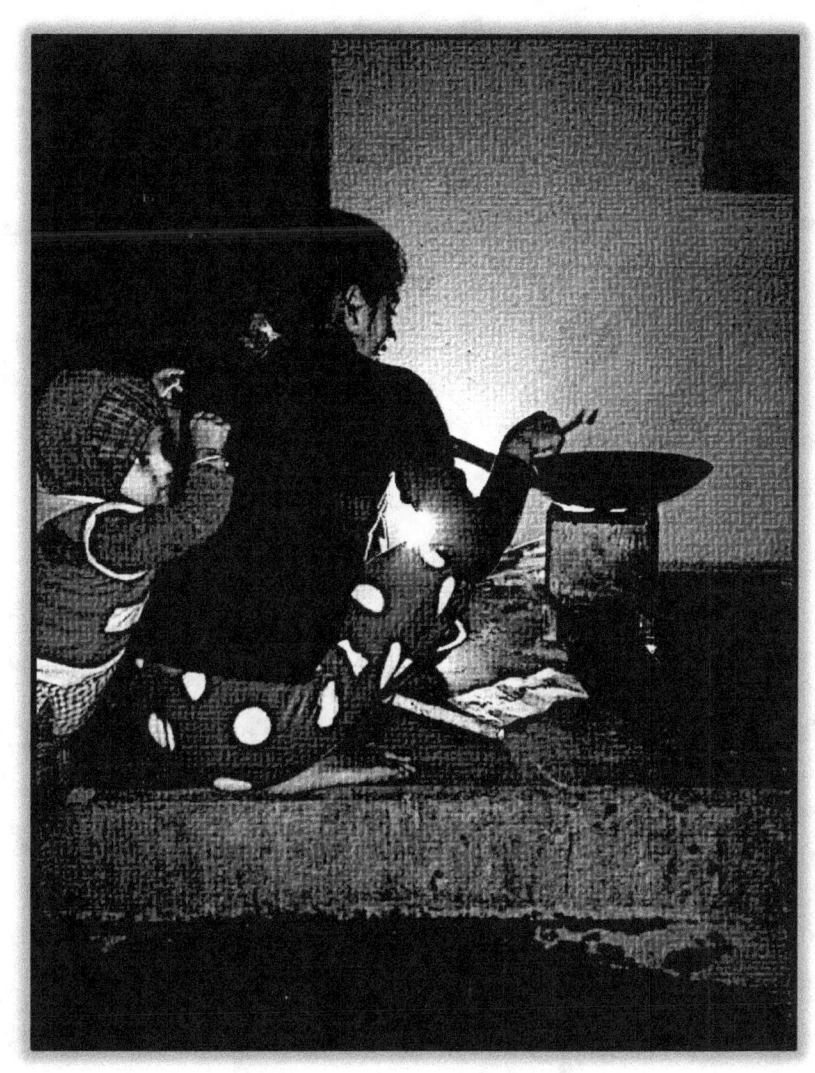

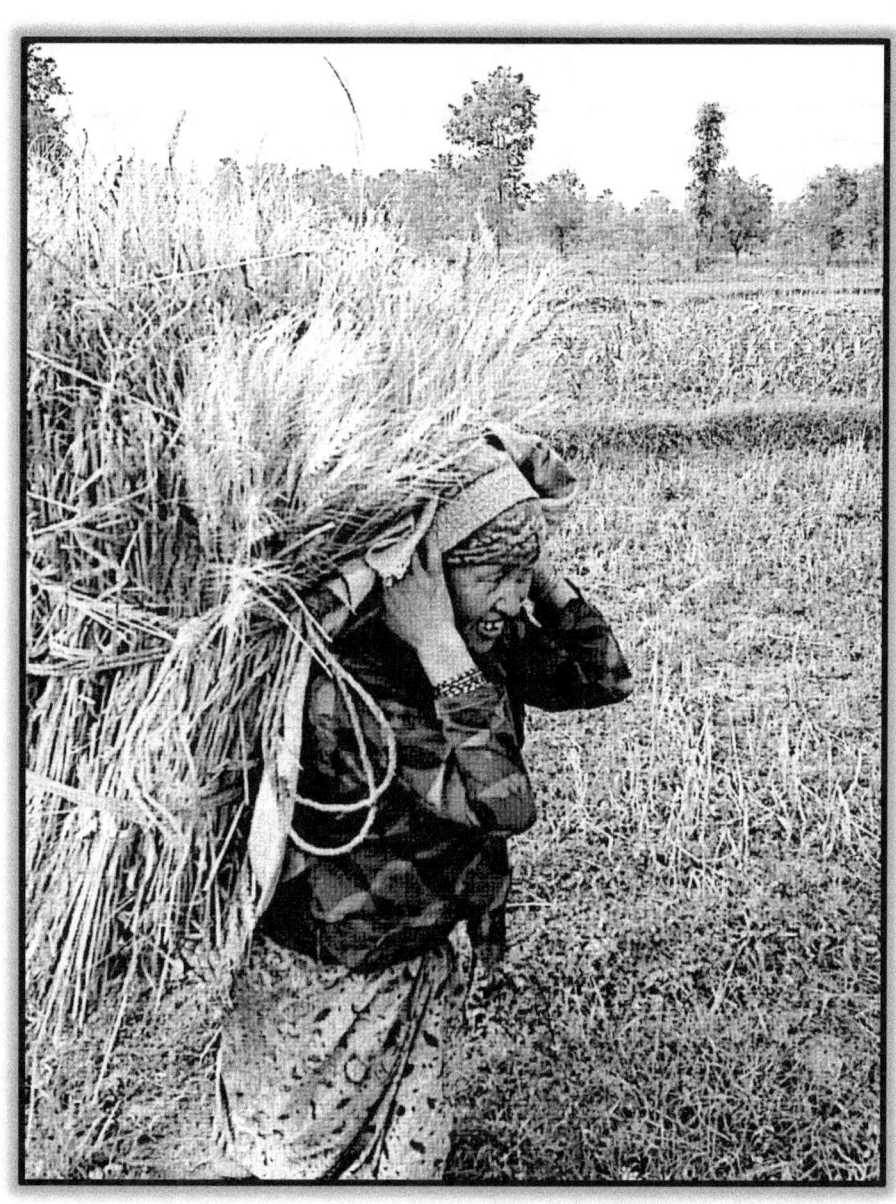

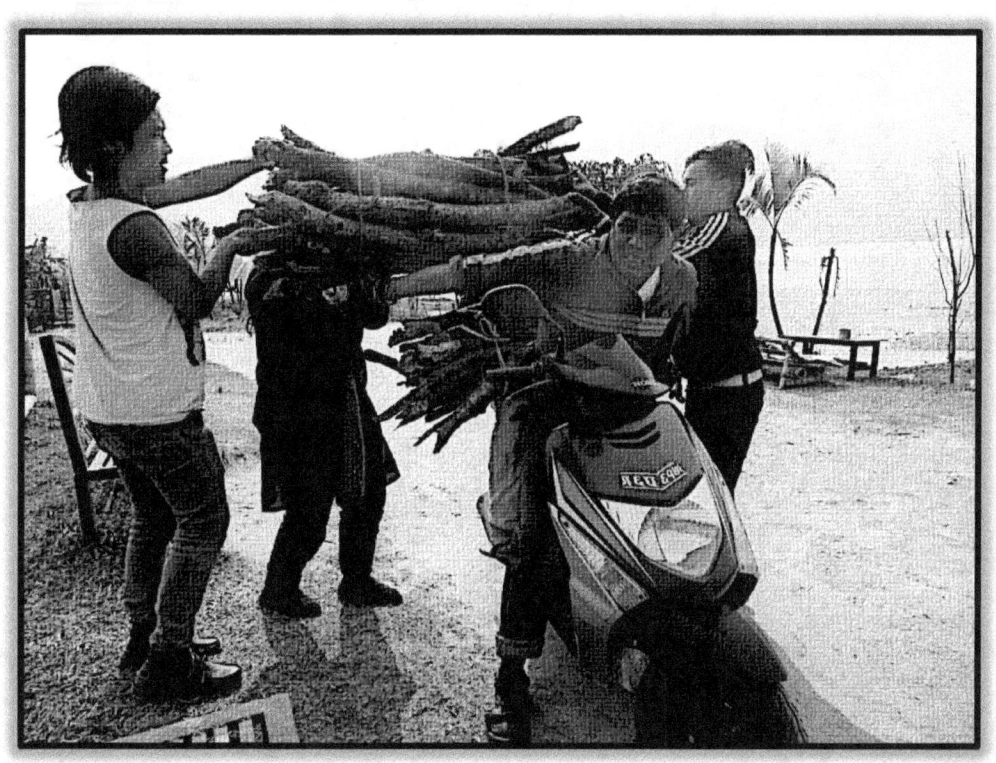

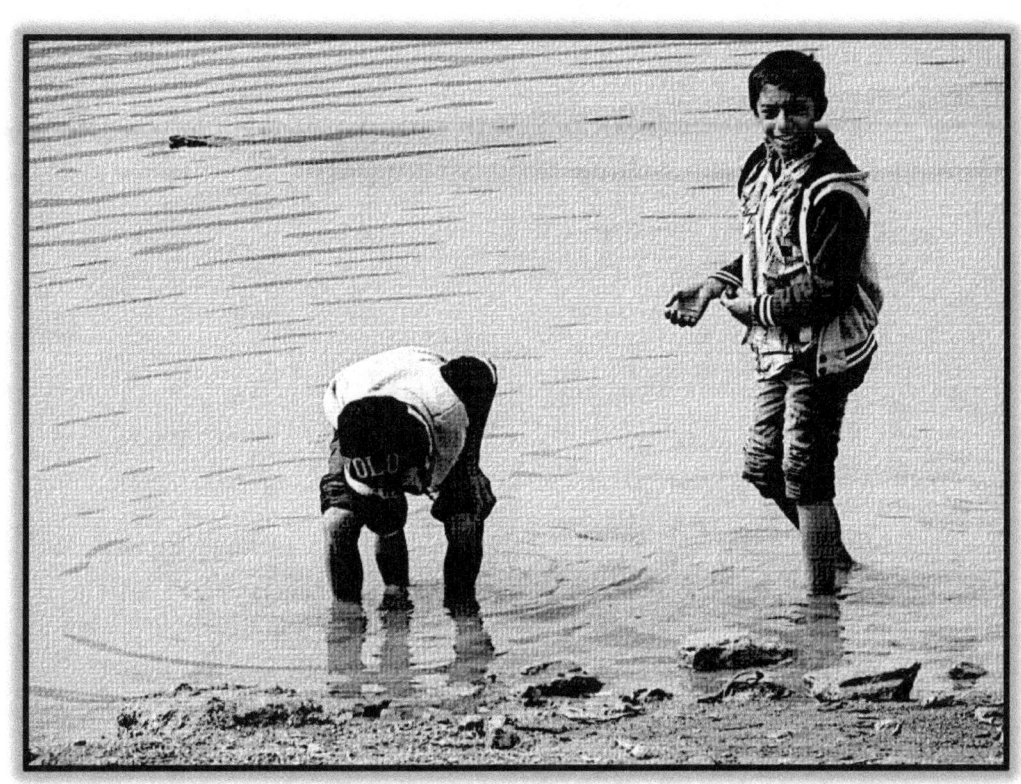

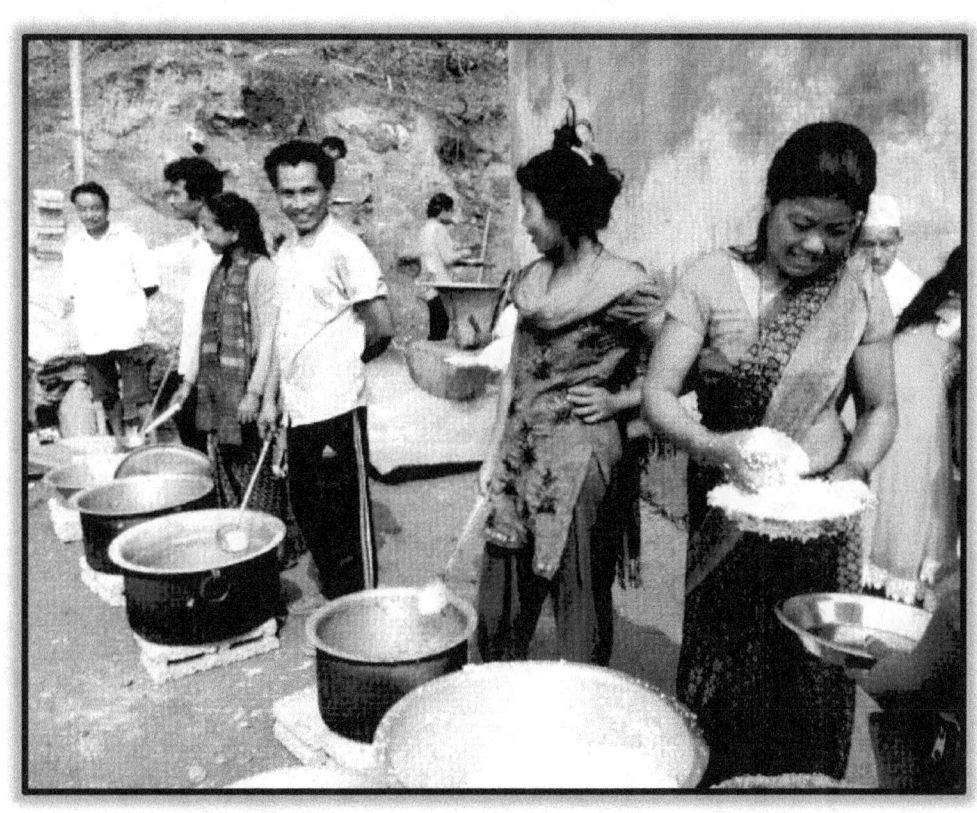

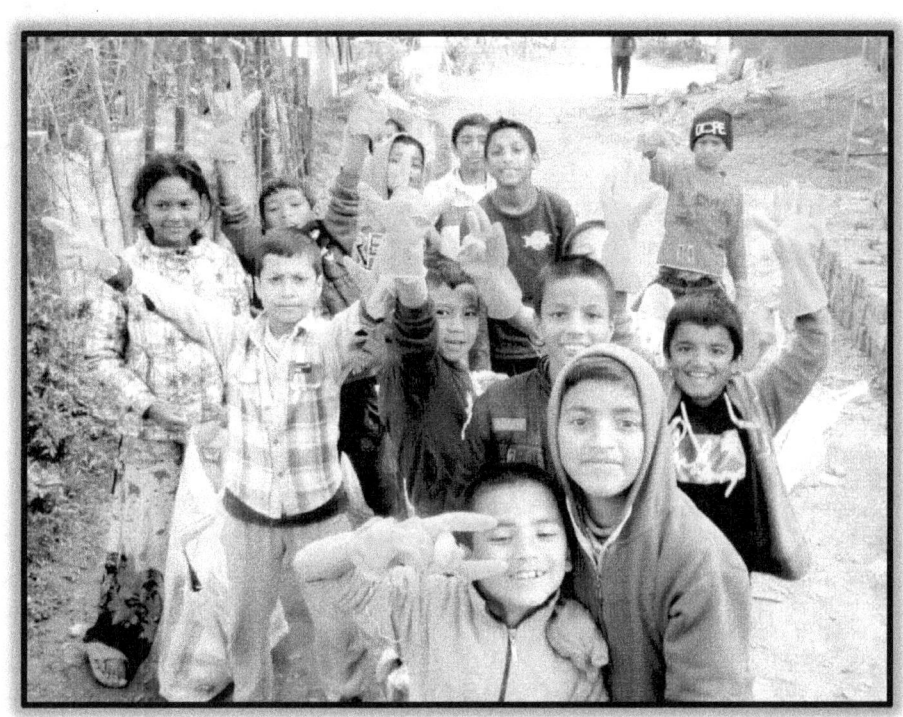

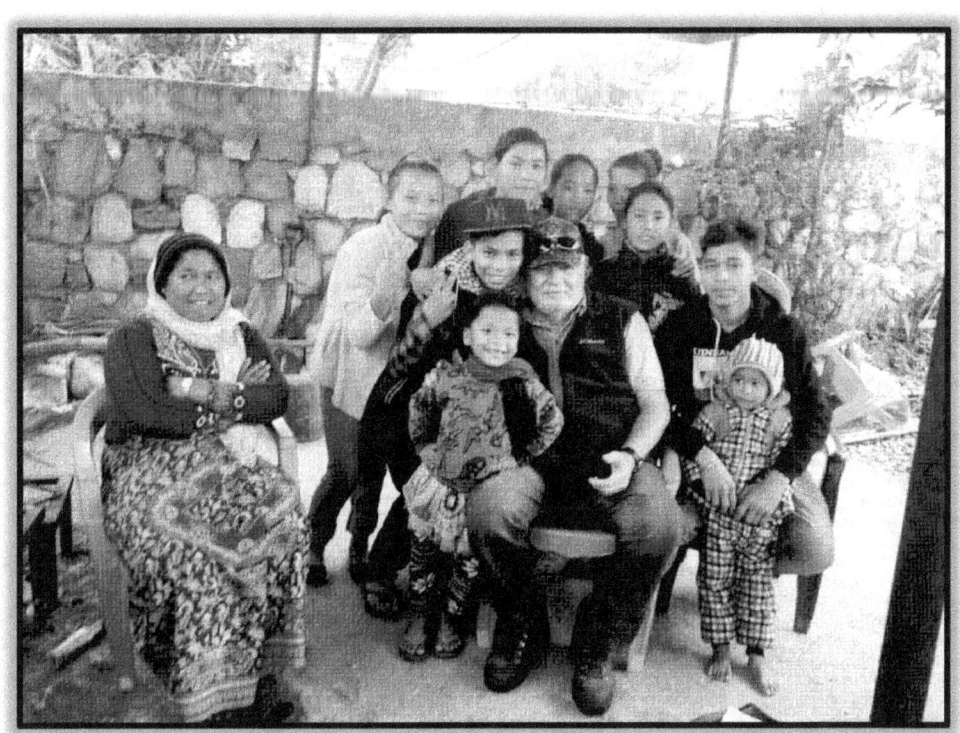

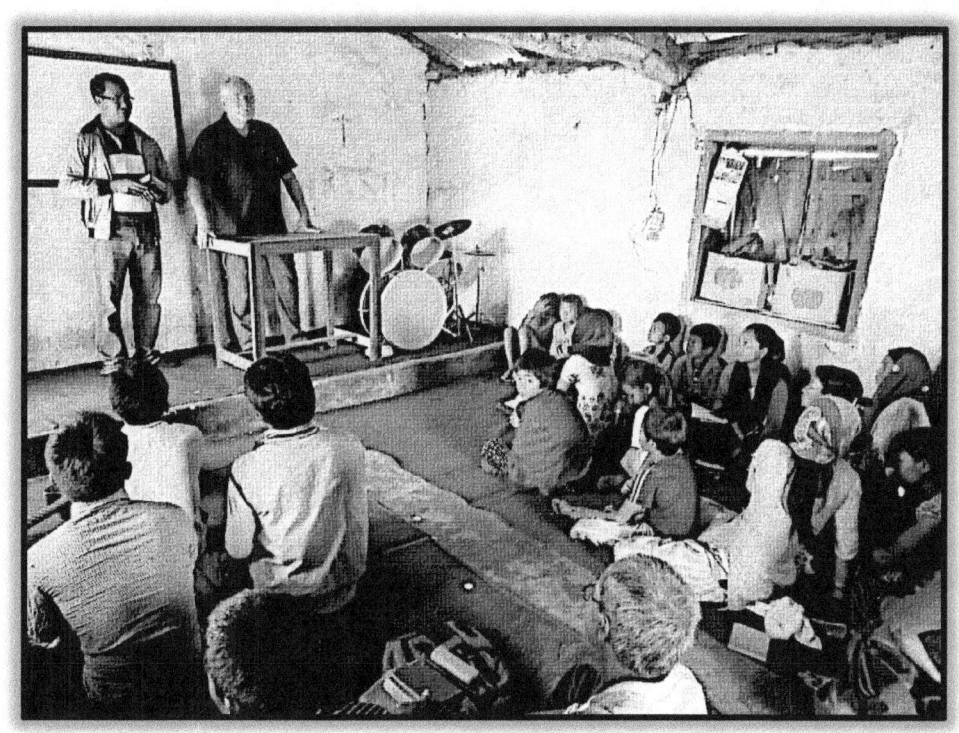

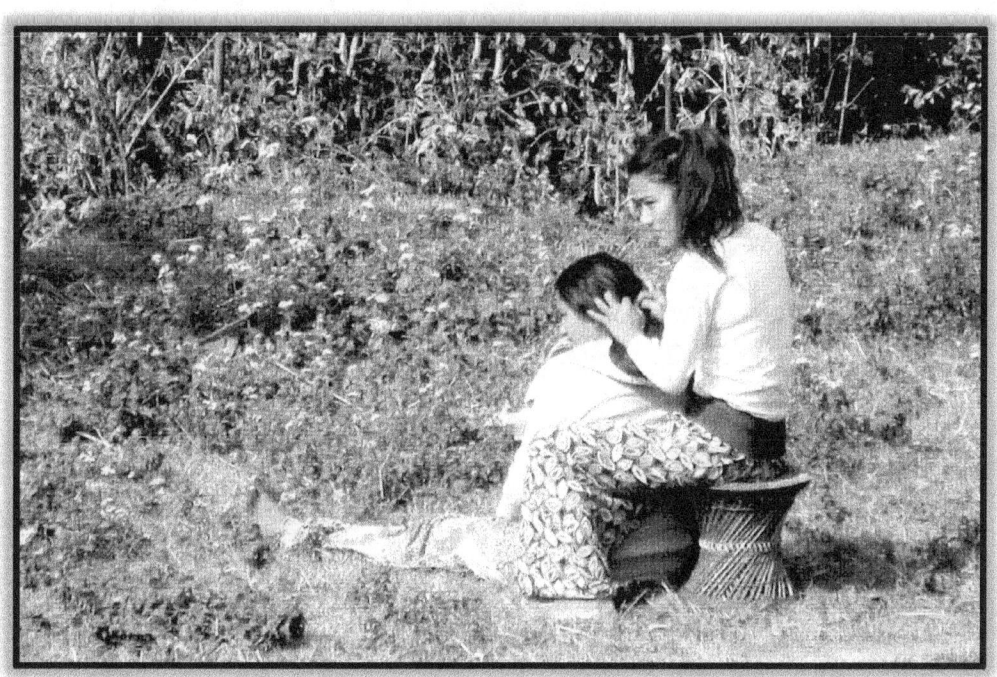

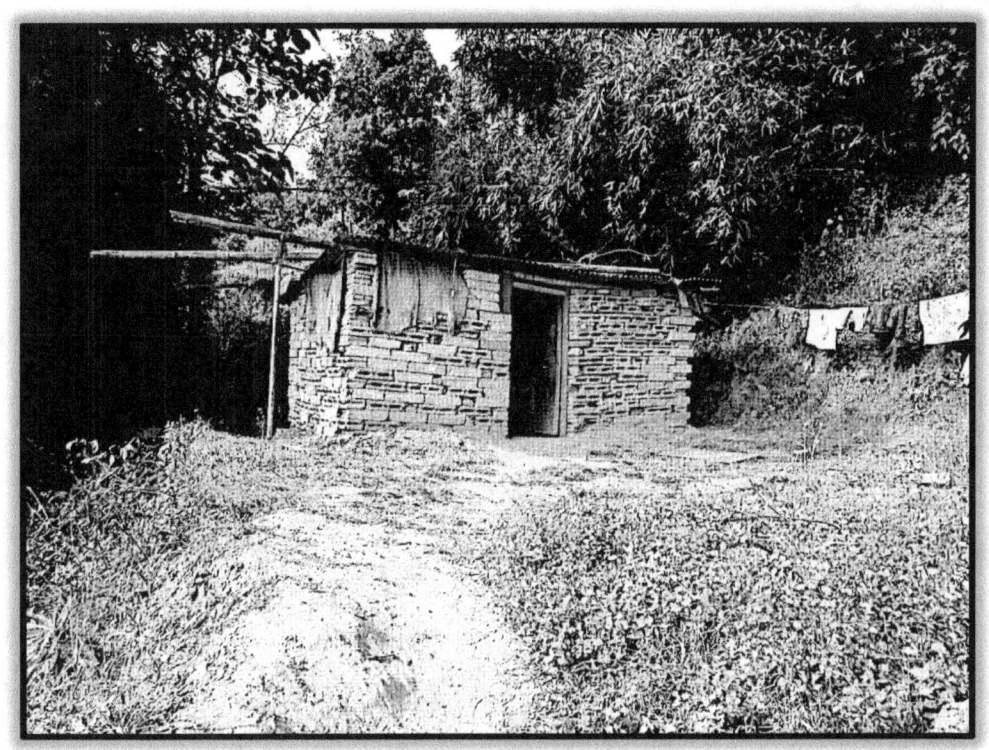

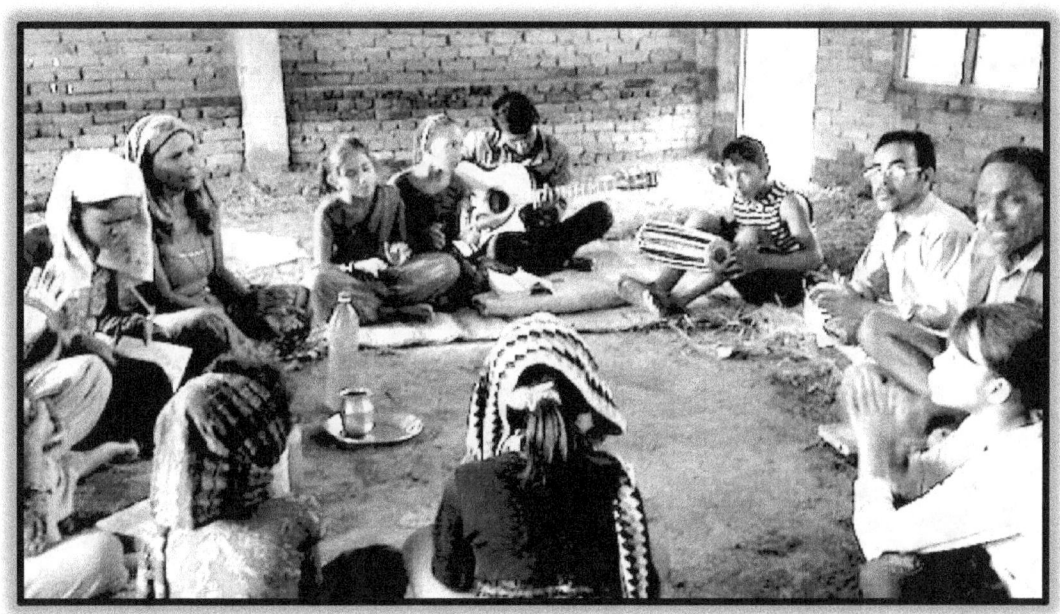

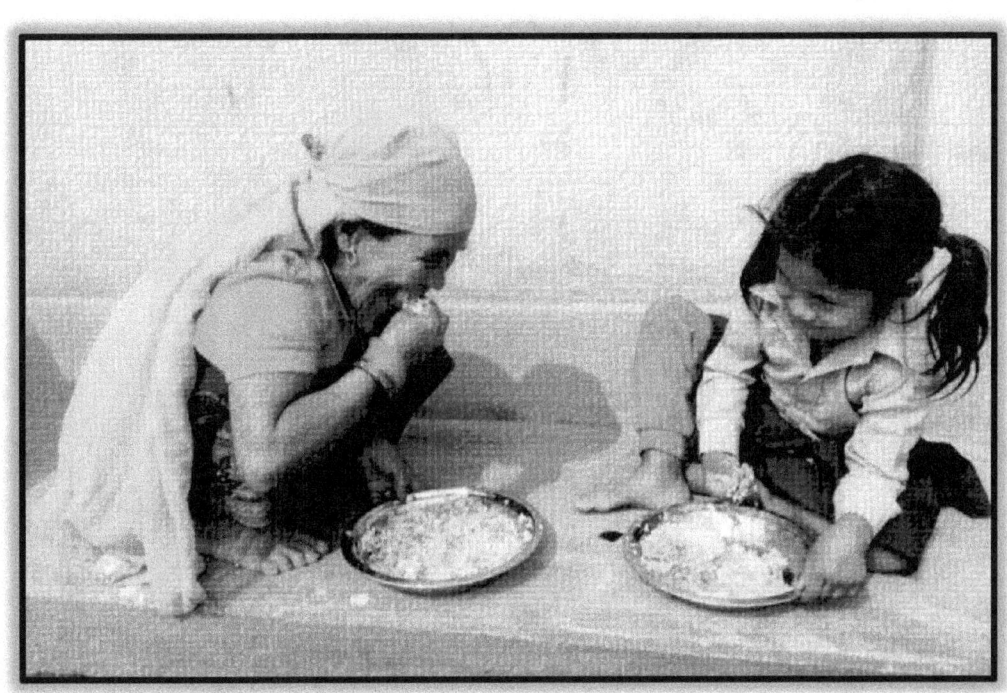

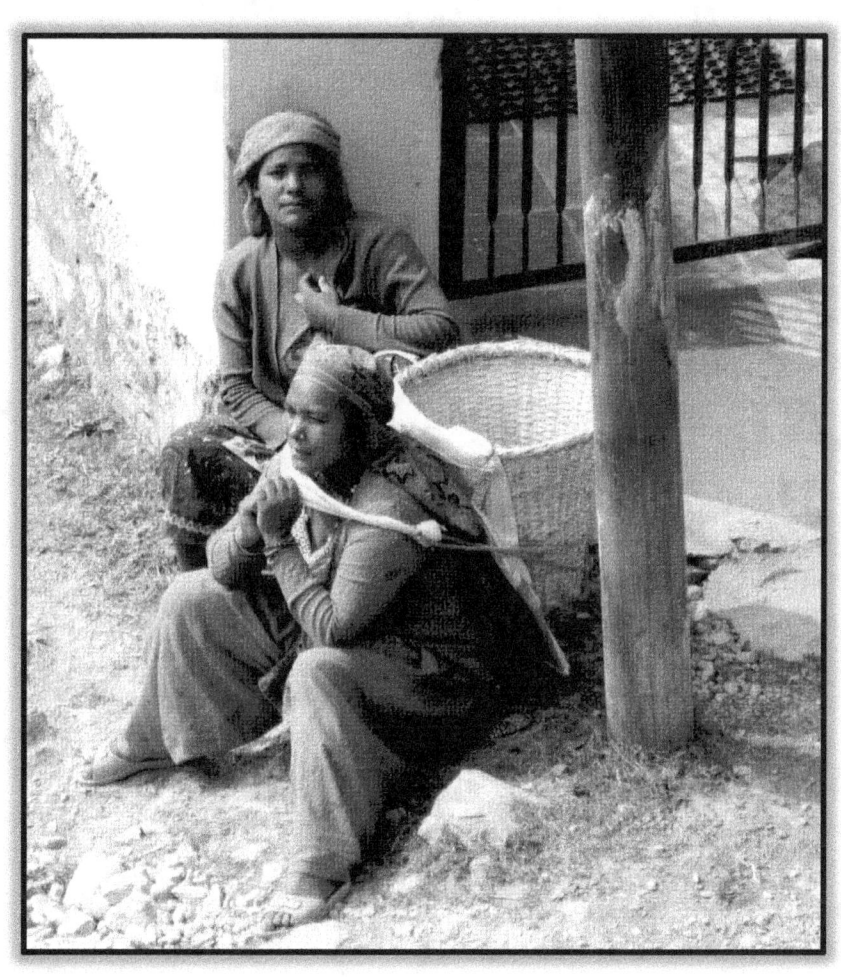

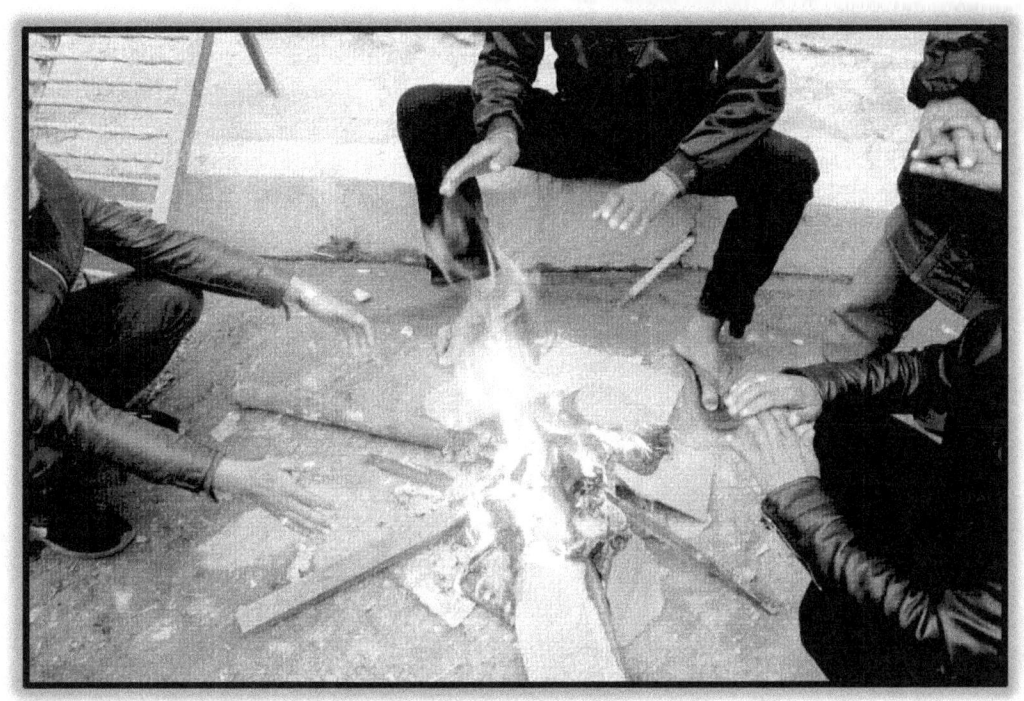

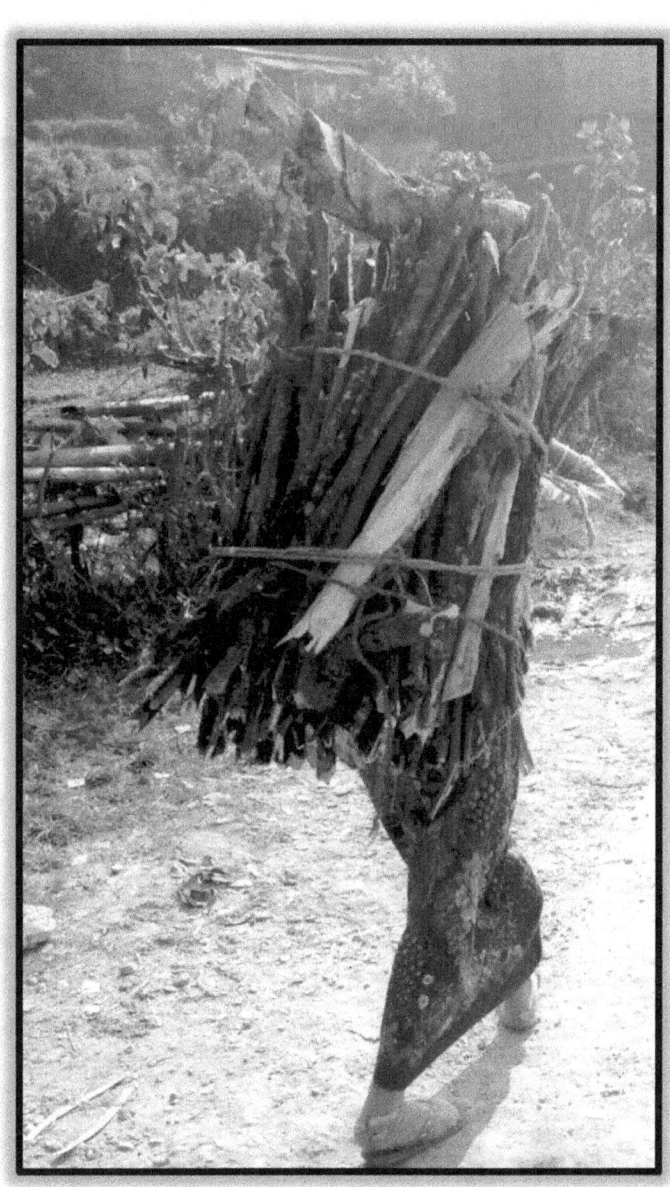

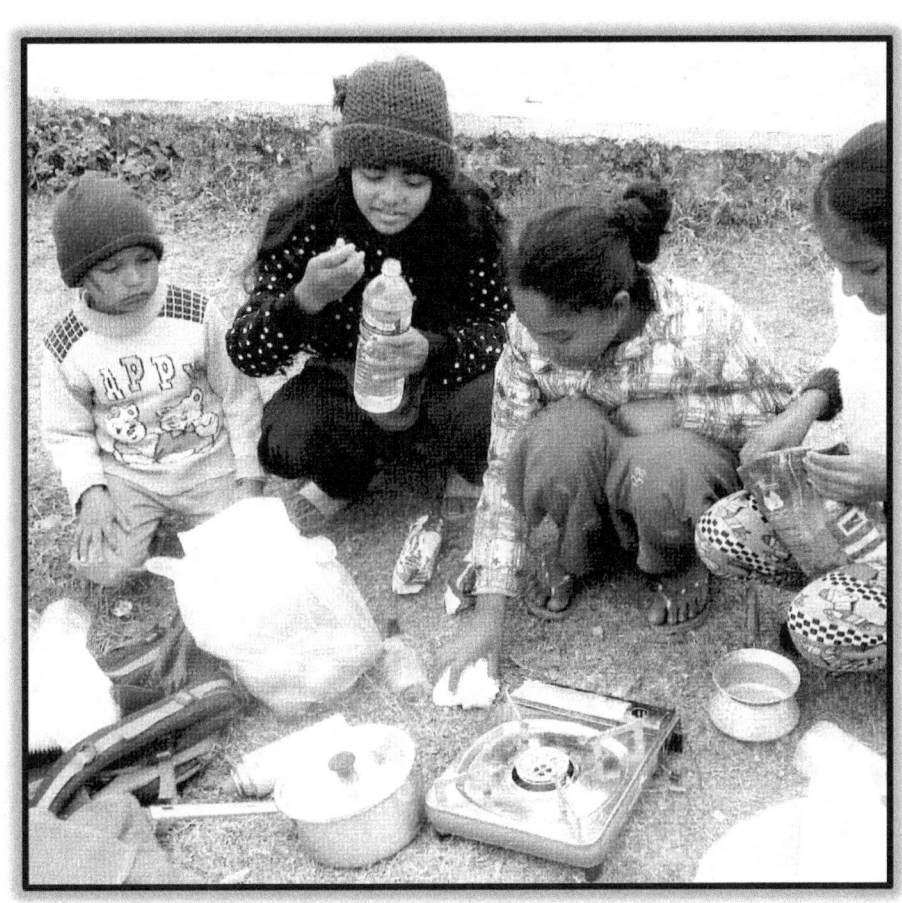

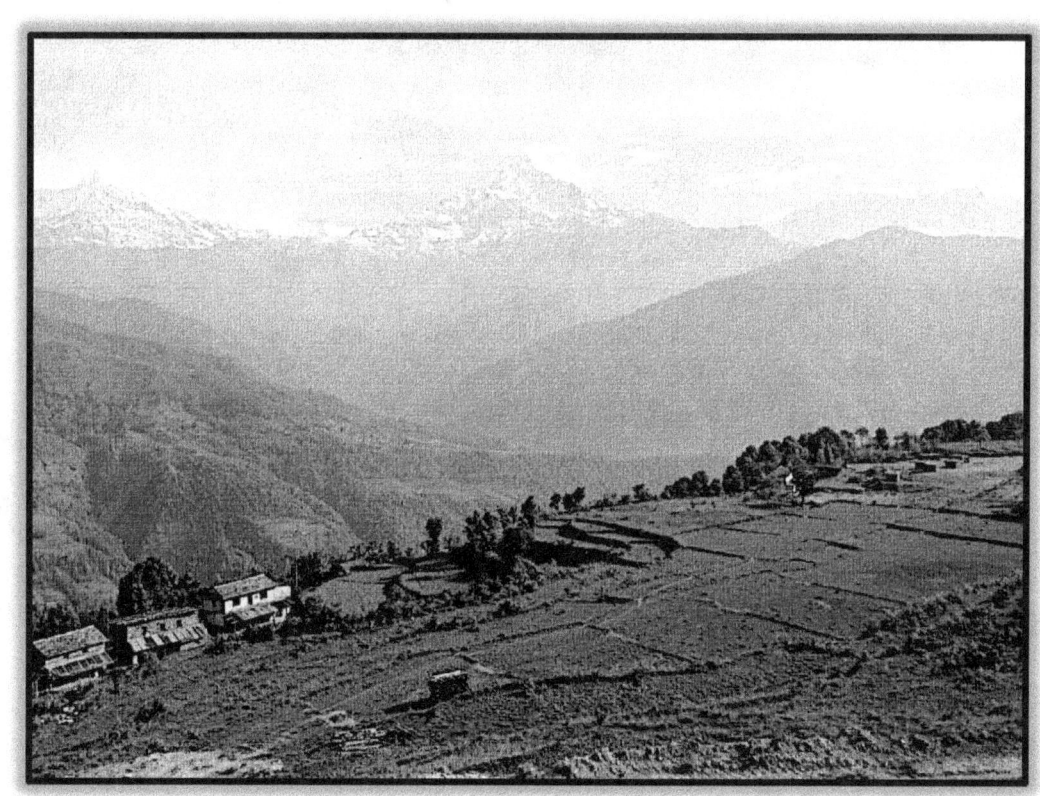

In Closing...

We are thankful to have been used to help in Nepal and the imagery in this book reminds us of just how grateful we are for having been born in a nation, the USA, that is so blessed and how fortunate we are to have so many friends in Nepal.

Many of the poor that we see every day in the United States are in that condition by fault of their own bad choices since so much opportunity is available for the diligent student and employee. And yes, there are also those who have been afflicted in life and need our help, but not near the high percentage of those in developing nations whose people live in poverty stricken lands brought about by oppressive governments, wars, natural disasters, diseases, lack of fresh water, food shortages, etc. We remain convinced that along with the physical help there needs to be the spiritual help for hearts and souls and minds and wills, provided by faith in Jesus Christ and we bring that truth wherever we go. The Bible verse that so fits us in recent years is Isaiah 58:10

"If you pour yourself out for the hungry and satisfy the desire of the afflicted, then shall your light rise in the darkness and your gloom be as noonday."

I never thought, in the vastness of my imagination, that I would write and publish a coloring book that could help the poor, yet here it is. Thank you for participating.

Kenny Reese Allen
Website - www.kennyreeseallen.com
Email – coffeetablecoloringbook@gmail.com

www.ingramcontent.com/pod-product-compliance
Lightning Source LLC
Chambersburg PA
CBHW081152180526

45170CB00006B/2035